42 Rules for Successful Collaboration

By David Coleman
Special Foreword by Mabel Casey

E-mail: info@superstarpress.com
20660 Stevens Creek Blvd., Suite 210
Cupertino, CA 95014

First Printing: May 2009
Second Printing: May 2010
Paperback ISBN: 978-1-60773-024-8 (1-60773-024-3)
Place of Publication: Silicon Valley, California, USA
Library of Congress Number: 2009925502
eBook ISBN: 978-1-60773-025-5 (1-60773-025-1)

Trademarks

All terms mentioned in this book that are known to be trademarks or service marks have been appropriately capitalized. Super Star Press™ cannot attest to the accuracy of this information. Use of a term in this book should not be regarded as affecting the validity of any trademark or service mark.

Warning and Disclaimer

Praise For This Book!

"Rarely is there a person who sees the future from 1000 feet and directs us all through the eye of the rising storm. David is one of those authors. I had the chance to cross paths with David in 2001 in the late teleconference days. Back then, e-learning was just a way to use conferencing technology. David insisted this virtual learning was more than just a virtual meeting—it was a whole new way to do business. And, he was right.

As publisher of E-Learning! Magazine, I have seen a lot of change over these 9 years. David Coleman, collaboration, Web 2.0 and e-learning are always crisscrossing. I am happy to have David as a sounding board, and think of him as a thought-provoking innovator of our industry. He may not design virtual world technology, but he shows us how to build this thing and use it to benefit our enterprises.

One day, we will all look back at what true collaborative technology did to our work process, and it will be like the day I tell my son about life before the Internet. No one will believe it. This book, '42 Rules for Successful Collaboration,' and the others to follow, will help us all forge a means to optimize technology within our work environments with less pain, thanks to David's efforts."
Catherine Upton, Publisher, E-Learning! Magazine

"Don't be shy about asking people on Twitter to spread the word for you. If they like what you do, they will. If they don't, they won't. It's as simple and transparent as that. If you don't ask, you don't get. Unfortunately (or perhaps fortunately for some of us), most people don't have the chutzpah to ask for help. David not only asked for help but got it and came up with a great book about collaboration. It does not have much about my favorite collaboration tool (Twitter) but is nevertheless a volume of collected wisdom about the topic."
Guy Kawasaki, Technology Evangelist, Blogger, and Entrepreneur

"David has brought together all the rules that will enable you to excel at the game of collaboration. Insightful, thought provoking, practical, pragmatic, focused, contemporary, and hands-on represent just a few of the terms that describe David Coleman's book, '42 Rules for Successful Collaboration.' Guaranteed, this book will not end up on your bookshelf collecting dust. You will keep this resource in your desk-after you have had each one of your colleagues read it (assuming you get it back from them). David and his contributing authors touch upon everything from soft skills to state-of-the-art collaborative technologies. When the rules are applied, your organization will rise to a new level of performance."
Don Straits, CEO, Cool Conference Live,
http://www.coolconferencelive.com

"In my 30 years in the software business, I have never seen a book about collaboration like this one. It not only collects the wisdom of many experts on collaboration worldwide, but actually uses collaboration to help to create the book itself. David reached out to his social networks for contributions, and has done a skillful job in editing and sequencing the rules in this book making it of great value to anyone who works with others both in the real or virtual worlds."
David Rolston, Ph.D., PE, CEO, Forterra Inc.

"Since I focus on social networks I was interested to hear from David that his new book on collaboration was written by one. I have heard of other experiments like with, where Guy Kawasaki had people add to his book online, but I don't think I had heard of anyone using their social network to write a book and actually get it done in a timely manner. Kudos to David for aggregating such a great collection of wisdom about collaboration. Not only will I blog about this book, but will recommend it to my social networks."
Susan Mernit, Blogger and Trouble Maker

"Based on 50 years as a Chief Procurement Officer, academic, consultant, author of eight books and creator of the 'Supply Chain Management Institute,' I know that there is an immense need for this practical and easy to read book! Collaboration is the key to successful and happy families, cooperation with friends and colleagues, collaborative organizations, and successful and profitable business-to-business relationships. Must reading."

David N. Burt, Ph.D., Emeritus Professor of Supply Chain Management, University of San Diego and author 8e. of "Supply Management"

"If anyone is poised to provide sage counsel in the form of 42 new rules of engagement, it is David Coleman. He was one of the first to recognize the power of collaborative—not competitive—advantage. He understands fundamentally that being innovative is not enough—especially in the current economic tsunami. Leadership is a function of innovation strategy. Turning clichés into sound counsel, he guides us into the new realm of virtual worlds—blogs, webinars and web conferencing. Simple—without being simplistic, David takes the mystery out of 21st Century communication."

Debra M. Amidon, Founder and CEO,
***Entovation* International Ltd.**

Dedication

This book is dedicated to all my social networks and all those who put in their time, effort and thought in contributing a rule for this groundbreaking book. This is a new way to write a book, a collaborative way that I think will be the blueprint for future books.

I also want to dedicate this book, to my wife Jennie. She is a great partner, proofreader, critic and supporter. Her unfailing belief in me is always an inspiration. She puts up with my long hours and unreasonable demands with a smile. This is my fourth book on collaboration, so I think she is getting used to my book writing process and understands that this is a great outlet for my creativity.

Acknowledgements

Publisher: Mitchell Levy, for your "let's make a deal attitude" as well as your encouragement and support for my ideas (which are pretty crazy sometimes).

Executive/Series Editor: Laura Lowell, Executive Editor for the 42 Rules series. Thanks for all your encouragement, guidance attention to detail and good humor.

Copy Editor: Suhag Shirodkar, thanks for your comments and guidance through this process.

Cover Design: Mark Elias

Layout: Pramod Rodrigues and Reshma Tendulkar, Teclarity

I wish to thank a large number of people whom I have had conversations with about collaboration in the enterprise over the last year. The conversations with you helped clarify my thinking, and made it easier to organize this book.

I wish to thank:

Oliver Marks – Collaboration 2.0 Blog ZDnet

Joe Wher – Executive coach

Susan Mernit – Blogger and troublemaker

Catherine Upton – Elearning magazine

Jay Cross – eLerning guru

Eilif Trondsen – Virtual worlds guru

Marc Gingras – CEO Tungle

Joe Ouye – Founder NewWow.net

Jim Creighton – Founder NewWow.net

Patricia Roberts – Jones, Lang, LaSalle

Dr. Renate Fruchter – Stanford University

Linda Stone – Generational guru

Stowe Boyd – Guru of everything

Maria Penaar – FinPro

Stewart Levine – Interpersonal skills guru

Sandy Vosk – Supply Chain Management guru

Ismael Ghalimi – Office 2.0

Mike Dressler – CommunityXperts

Bob Sayle – CommunityXperts

Dave Antila – Technical expert

Russell Cox – Executive and Internet coach

Manish Sood – CEO C-mail

Russell Mix – Qtask

Tim Young – CEO Socialcast

Pekka Parnanen – Finnode

Ross Mayfield – SocialText

Maureen Jennings – O'Rielly

Aaron Fulkerson – CEO Mindtouch

Kate North and all the folks at Haworth

Amy Wohl – Analyst extrordinnare

All the Lotusphere folks from IBM/Lotus

All the folks at Cutter IT (Karen, Cindy, Anne, etc.)...

and all the collaboration vendors, researchers and pundits who continue to educate me.

Contents

Special Foreword by Mabel Casey

As a leader in the design and manufacture of office furniture and interior architecture, Haworth knows that collaboration is one of the many tools and techniques critical for effective working. We are presenting this special edition of *42 Rules for Successful Collaboration* to help you understand how critical collaboration is to your future and provide some practical guidelines for your success.

You will find many helpful nuggets of wisdom on collaboration in David's book. From my perspective and experience, here are a few that held special significance:

- Mismatching of common context and experience can happen within local teams but often is even more extreme on global teams when team members are from different cultures, and maybe even different companies. In Rule 3 David talks about trust and how trust is often seen as the foundation of collaboration. But, in a global team example, it may not be enough. Understanding the local context of each team member is critical to the success of the team project. Rules 5-7 examine this, suggesting active inclusion and providing a structure or methodology to do this type of communication in a productive way.

- I coach managers around the world and have found Rule 11 to be very important. Put simply: "who says it" is often as important as "what is said." An analogy I have often used is, "You may believe you have thrown out a BB, but the recipient feels like they have caught a cannonball." It is easy to forget that when you are in a position of power, people automatically add weight to anything you say. You may be "thinking out loud," but others interpret your comments as a directive. It is important to always consider how your input will be perceived. How requests are communicated is critical to collaboration success.

- As leaders, we have to set the example and expectations. Rule 16 discusses a culture of candor. My interpretation of this is to communicate in the same context, understand the same goals, and be in personal alignment with corporate goals and initiatives. Spending some extra time on this in the beginning can save you a great deal of time (and money) in the end.

I personally believe that collaboration is an essential element to success in today's world. I hope that this book gives you new insight and tools to fuel your interactions and that you enjoy it as much as I did!

Mabel Casey
Vice President of Global
Marketing and Sales Support
Haworth, Inc.

Why would I write another book on collaboration when I just released one last year (Collaboration 2.0 with co-author Stewart Levine)? Anything to do with Web 2.0 and Social Networks is hot right now. I want to be clear—collaboration is a human behavior, not a technology or a process but an act or series of acts that you choose to perform with one or more people (through the computer) to accomplish a specific purpose or goal. This is my fourth book on collaboration, and I believe the most easy to read.

I have often talked about the "Mom Test" in my writing; what I mean by this is if a collaborative application is easy enough for my Mom to use (she is smart and well educated but did not grow up with computers) then it passes the "Mom Test." Glance,[1] a screen sharing collaboration tool passed the Mom Test, whereas WebEx (now Cisco) did not. My goal is to have this book be an easy enough to read to pass the "Mom Test."

My first two books (published by Prentice Hall) were also contributed volumes, but they were much more academic (I think all Prentice Hall books end up looking like text books!) and much longer (600–700 pages). My mom took one quick look through them and asked, "Do I have to read this?" At that point I knew these books had not passed the "Mom Test." Although they were popular in undergraduate and graduate-level classes on collaboration, they were not easily read by the uninitiated.

Collaboration 2.0, which was itself a collaborative effort (between Stewart Levine and myself) and used a variety of collaboration tools to help with the writing and publication of the book. Collaboration 2.0 was meant to be a more

---

1. http://www.glance.net

approachable book (and only 300 pages) as well as a more balanced one. I asked Stewart, who has more expertise in interpersonal communications and interactions, to write part of the book and bring more "people" into a book mostly about "process" and "technology."

We use the same holistic model (People, Process and Technology) in this book, but the format is designed for a different audience. The 42 Rules format helps break up this collective wisdom into bite sized and easily digestible chunks. So you could read only one rule (written in plain English) and still take something of value from the book, without reading anything else. Of course I encourage you to read all 42 rules, but it is my hope that this book will now pass the "Mom Test." After all, it is best to lead by example, and since I advise a lot of collaboration tool vendors and start-ups, and am always on them about making their software more approachable and easy, I thought my book should follow those principles also.

This book is not only different in format, but is unique in the way it was written. I decided to "walk my talk," and ask for input from the many groups, communities and social networks I am in, and make this a collaborative effort. Not that my three earlier books were not also a collaborative effort, but I never used a social network to help write them. To start this effort, I posted a question on LinkedIn asking, "What is your best advice around Collaboration?" I got many replies, and some of them were so good that I included them in this book. So it really has been a collaborative effort.

I also have a good relationship with Mitchell Levy, publisher of HappyAbout titles and co-publisher, with Laura Lowell, of the 42 Rules book series through Super Star Press. Both these relationships have been collaborative and have both added to this book and to my life.

1 Rules Are Meant to Be Broken

The 42 Rules book series differs fundamentally from other non-fiction business books. The writing, publishing, distribution, and marketing approaches for this series have all broken rules in order to build something unique, flexible and fast.

I talked with Mitchell and Laura in November of 2008 and told them of my idea to write this book, and how I wanted to approach it. I put out a call for rules before Thanksgiving, and gave a due date of 1/1/09 (which I missed by a month). I ended up writing 10 rules in this book and have about 30 contributors, many of whom I have never met in person. Some contributors are in my personal or professional networks, some are on LinkedIn or on my mailing list. Others are academic or research colleagues. If I had received rules from all those who said they would send one (or more) in, I would have enough for a Volume II.

Many of the rules sent in were not in the right format or did not project the right message and so were sent back to their authors (some several times). By the end of January, I had turned in my first draft of the book and over the next four months, and went through the publishing process with Super Star Press and HappyAbout, with the book coming out in May 2009. All told, seven months from start to finish.

Since I published my first book with Prentice Hall in 1995, the technology for publishing has changed radically (unfortunately, many publishers have not). In the old process you needed an "agent" who will negotiate an advance for you from a publisher who accepts your book idea or manuscript. These publishers are something of an "old boys' network" and once you are in, you are in, but often it takes a great deal of effort to be a member of this club.

I have never had an agent, and tend to follow a philosophy proposed by that greatest of philosophers, Groucho Marx, when he said, "I refuse to join any club that would have me as a member." My first two books took 18 months to come out once I had submitted the manuscript. The problem with this slow process is that the technology I was writing about (collaboration technologies) was changing very rapidly (and still are), and the books were out of date before they were printed.

I learned that, whatever the process, it is really up to the author to do the marketing and drive interest for the book. Even from the more traditional publishers I never got a marketing budget or a publicist for my books. Mitchell and Laura were both supportive in marketing along with having a well oiled machine for getting books quickly through the publishing process. Mitchell was always there if I came up with a different or new idea for marketing my books, and listened patiently, brainstormed with me, so that we eventually came up with new and successful ways to market my books.

Section I
People

I have divided the book into three sections to help with the organization of the rules. This first section has rules about collaboration that mostly apply to people, their behaviors and interactions. An underlying theme is the use of Web 2.0 tools and technologies to enable the interactions that are so critical for success. The rules focus on why you are collaborating, who to trust and who you are collaborating with.

These are followed by rules about communication and conflict. The final and largest section in this book are rules about how to be successful with collaboration that go from a culture of professional candor to celebration of specific collaborative interactions.

2 Know Why You Are Collaborating

Another way of looking at this question is to ask yourself, "What are the business behaviors my organization needs to have in order to achieve the results I am looking for?"

Jeff Young is a collaborative learning facilitator and coach. Jeff wrote this rule because most potential clients he talks with are interested in collaboration but have trouble articulating, to peers or to management, what they want to improve through collaboration. This lack of clarity results in a much lower success rate in initially funding the collaborative effort and in keeping it adequately funded over time.

This may seem like a very obvious and perhaps even silly rule. Yet I find that most people and most organizations I have met with have very different ideas about the meaning of collaboration. Many think that collaboration is a touchy-feely and weak approach while others think it is just about offering technology to aid communication—like a fancy telephone. While the meaning of collaboration is fuzzy, what seems to be even fuzzier is why they want to collaborate in the first place.

When I have asked clients why they are collaborating, most of the responses I received were similar to the following:

- **To reduce costs:** My training budget was slashed and I have to find a way of bringing a dispersed workforce together to get vital training on much less money, so I invested in collaboration technology.

- **To reduce travel and time away from work:** We hold weekly sales meetings that are critical to the success of our business and we have grown to a point where it is taking them too long away from critical clients for everyone to come by every week to get the latest strategy or share ideas.

- **We can't get everyone into the same room at the same time:** Everyone's calendar is so jammed that it has become impossible to get everyone together at the same time.

- **Because we want to involve everyone in the company:** It is a personal value of mine to include everyone in the important decision-making of the company. It makes everyone feel good about working for this company.

While these responses seem to be answering my question in a very direct and reasonable way, I have noticed something importantly similar about them. The reasons all seem to be formed from a similar mindset described by this generic statement: *"We are used to doing _____ in our business, and things have changed to a point where we need to find a way to support our interactions so we can keep doing it in spite of the changes."* The responses tend to be ones that are desires to keep doing the same actions we are used to, not really getting at the business reasons for *why* we want to collaborate.

Another way of looking at this question is to ask yourself, *"What are the business behaviors my organization needs to have in order to achieve the results I am looking for?"* When I know what specific business results I am looking for and that collaboration is a critical behavior I can tie directly to achieving my results, *then* I know why I want to collaborate.

It is rare that I run into a client who responds to my "why" question with a response like, *"Because we need to increase our revenue by $4 million next year and I want to come together with my customers and suppliers to figure out together how we can increase our value to the marketplace to earn that increase in revenue."* When I get a response like that, it is very clear to me why they want to collaborate and whether the investment in collaboration is worth the time, effort, and money to make it happen.

Trust Is Not Enough!

What I came to realize is that, for collaboration to be successful, trust does help, but understanding the "local context" of your team members was even more critical.

Other contributors with rules in this book will tell you that trust is the cornerstone of collaboration. However, in my 20 years of working with teams I have seen some teams where the members don't trust each other, yet they do collaborate if they have a common goal. So what is really required for successful collaboration?

For many years I thought trust was critical for collaboration or for distributed teams to be effective, but after attending the NewWOW (New ways of working: http://www.newwow.net) symposium in the Summer of 2008 which looked at the effects of culture, I began to understand that trust was just not enough. Also, I can easily think of situations where people on a team or committee did not trust each other yet worked together for a common goal. Just look at any standards committee for a good example of this.

From Wikipedia: Trust is *a relationship of reliance.*

> *It does not need to involve belief in the good character, vices, or morals of the other party. And it does not need to include an action that you and the other party are mutually engaged in. In fact, trust is a **prediction** of reliance on an action, based on what a party knows about the other party.*
> http://tinyurl.com/6xa2w3 [2]

---

2. en.wikipedia.org/wiki/Trust_(social_sciences)

What I came to realize is that for collaboration to be successful, trust does help, but understanding the "local context" of your team members was even more critical. What I mean by "local context" is knowing about the other team members, the organizations they are in, the country culture and their individual characteristics. Without an understanding of this local context, poor communication and missed meanings run rampant on distributed teams; especially teams with members from "high context" cultures (like Japan) when they are intermixed with team members from "low context" cultures (like the U.S.).

A good example of this occurred when I conducted some classes on collaboration in Japan a few years ago. The classes went well and when I got back to the U.S., I emailed my main contact in Japan to discuss some unresolved issues from the training. I also wanted to introduce them to others in the U.S. who I thought could benefit their business. I made an online (email) introduction and assumed everything was proceeding.

But that was not the case. My contact in Japan was not even replying to my emails. Finally in frustration I called my contact in Japan and asked what was going on. Now, I come from NY and have been told I can be rather straightforward, part of being from a low context culture. However, my contact in Japan was from a high context culture, one that also avoids conflict. He had enough trust in me to tell me that the introduction was being ignored because it had gone to the wrong people, and they lost "face" by it. Once I sent the email to my contact's boss, and asked permission for the introduction, things went a lot better. The boss "saved face," my contact was allowed to email me again, and the introduction was made.

How many times has something like this tripped you up when working on a geographically distributed and cross cultural team? I almost always recommend to my clients that the first team or project meeting should be in person (then it is much easier to do the electronic collaboration that follows) because it helps all the team members understand the local context for each other. This in-person visit, although expensive, should have some social experiences thrown in, as they help to speed up understanding (and possibly trust) of the other team members.

I found that taking the time in the beginning to learn about and know each of the other team members paid off in spades later on. Also the agreement on clear team processes and interactions at the beginning of a project also really paid off. Yes, both of these help to develop trust, but more than that, they give you an understanding of those you are working with, which is even more critical when you work at a distance.

You *Will* Include All of Your Stakeholders

What I didn't know then was there are important ways that we could have included all of the stakeholders without creating a really large group of equal decision makers.

Jeff Young is a collaborative learning facilitator and coach. He wrote this rule because many of his clients are focused on timely and effective decision-making and then find out the implementation of their decisions get bogged down or fail entirely.

Many years ago I heard a statement from someone that went something like this: *You **will** include all of your stakeholders on important decisions that affect them. You can either invite them early to an opportunity to learn from each other or you can fight with them later. Your choice!*

Here are two sample conversations and simple steps that help to make sure you not only include all your stakeholders, but you have a team small enough to make decisions.

Conversation 1: Information Gathering

1. What is it that you need to know to effectively make your decisions?
2. Who needs to be part of those conversations?
3. What do you need to learn from those stakeholders?

Making the Decision:

There are many ways of making a decision as a group. In one of the most widely read Harvard Business Review articles, Robert Tannenbaum and Warren Schmidt offer a model that defines seven different distinct styles of decision-making. These styles are:

- Makes decisions and announces the result.
- Makes a decision and sells it.
- Presents ideas, invites questions.
- Presents tentative decisions.
- Gets suggestions, then makes a decision.
- Defines limits and allows the group to make the decision.
- The group functions within limits defined by a manager.

If you want to know more you can consult "How to Choose a Leadership Pattern" in Harvard Business Review 36(2), pages 95–101.

Conversation 2: The Results

Once you have gained whatever learning you needed from your stakeholders and made your decisions based upon one of the seven decision making styles above, you need to go back to your stakeholders and share with them what you learned and the decisions made. The point of this second conversation is to provide inclusion and identify any person who cannot live with and support this decision. It isn't about whether everyone likes the decision—there will always be those who do not.

But you really have to demonstrate that you want to hear different points of view. After all, this is your only opportunity to learn more about any resistance that exists to implementation. How can you then incorporate the point of view of the resistance into your plans? If so, you will have a better decision and smoother implementation.

We usually resort to small decision making bodies because we want to make decisions quickly—but the real question is how quickly can you implement your decision? If you aren't including your stakeholders early you will take even longer implementing your decision than it takes to include them in the first place.

5 Actively Include Each Person on a Global Team

Actively include each person in the collaborative team's work.

Jane E. Smith, Esq., Founder and President of LiSimba Consulting Services, Inc., is an international executive coach, writer, and speaker, focusing on understanding cultural perspectives as they function in collaborative global work settings.

Collaboration is integral to meeting the goals of each task in our global working world. The team needs the open marketplace of ideas, which comes from the input of each participant. Each contribution offers unique views of the issue. The group's task can then be accomplished through open discussion of the many contributions. Sometimes the collaboration will be virtual as the team is spread across continents or all across the world. When we cannot "see" each other face to face, or when we can but there are many cultures represented on the team, collaboration across national boundaries and cultures can result in losing one or more participant's contributions. With each such loss, the lost person can feel removed from feeling a part of the team. In addition the team loses that person's perspectives and the potential that those perspectives bring to the task.

For example, I worked with a collaborative management team based in Mexico City. The team was led by an American (who reported to the parent corporation in the U.S.), and one of its tasks was to assure the regular delivery of raw materials to the manufacturing plant in Monterrey. The Chinese representative team member handled procurement for Mexico operations. The Dane was the operations engineer. The British team member dealt with finances, and the Mexican member was responsible for human resources for the manufacturing facility.

Unfortunately, deliveries of raw materials were two grades lower than what the Chinese member and his team had procured. At a team meeting the Danish member reported the slowdown in operations. He felt that the team should go straight to the management of the supplier in charge of the sub grade materials and perhaps shorten the down time in the operation. The Chinese member was horrified that the team would not go through the proper channels to solve the problem. For him, bypassing the hierarchy was unthinkable. Being from a western culture, the Briton agreed with the Dane and wanted to bypass the hierarchy and save delay costs. The Mexican member was more in line with the Chinese member, believing that the proper channels should be followed. In bypassing the hierarchy the Chinese member could lose face with his supplier contacts. The Mexican member could feel threatened as he too valued each communication channel and felt more secure knowing the line of authority.

The American manager, as team facilitator, had to choose the team direction (bypass or not to bypass). For him it would be easy to bypass the hierarchy to solve the problem as quickly as possible. But he knew that by not honoring the Mexican and the Chinese team members' aversion to bypassing hierarchy, the team could lose their active participation. The American talked privately with the Chinese about concerns and perspectives. Together they forged a way to deal directly with the problem supplier, with the Chinese member bringing the solution to the collaborative team. The team knew that the Chinese member had an excellent relationship with the suppliers. With the Chinese member leading the way, the low grade materials were removed. Proper grade materials were delivered in a timely manner. Each team member felt they participated and worked collaboratively for a successful outcome.

6

Being a Conscious Communicator Supports Successful Collaboration

For successful collaboration, get clear on the meaning of words.[3]

Stewart Levine has a 20-year practice in helping people to communicate with each other better. He is a great practitioner of communication to support successful collaborations.

Although it has some caveats, a 1967 study by Albert Mehrabian and Susan Ferris published in The Journal of Consulting Psychology revealed that about 90 percent of the message we get in a face-to-face (F2F) interaction is through tone of voices, and visual cues. Only about 10 percent of the information we get from other people is based on the content of what they say.

Today globalization of business, the movement towards geographically distributed and cross cultural teams, and the increasing number of people working from home is a fact of life. The way people interact, produce and collaborate has changed dramatically. The frequency and availability of F2F communication has been dramatically curtailed either by the rising cost of fuel or by travel bans in a variety of multinational organizations. What this means is the 10 percent that was information about content, is now 100 percent of the information a team member may get through interacting with you virtually. With

---

3. Let's Get Real or Let's Not Play: The Demise of Dysfunctional Selling and the Advent of Helping Clients Succeed/Mahan Khalsa, 1999, Franklin Covey Co. Printed by White Water Press

this situation in mind you need to be very conscious about what you say, when you say it and how you say it to your team members.

Below are three best practices (with examples) of conscious communication and how they can best be applied to distributed teams or distance collaboration:

1. **Build an Environment of Trust:** Although David says, "Trust is not enough" in Rule 3, I believe that trust is one of the most critical elements of effective distance communications. To create an environment of trust often requires the team leader to set an example for this behavior. This may be from offering open and transparent communication with other team members, or just a communication style that supports the free sharing of information between team members. One of the ways to do this and compensate for the lower bandwidth of communication is to increase the bandwidth of what you say. Don't assume everyone understands exactly what you say. Try to embellish on what you are saying and often see each communication as a way to tell a story.

2. **Set Expectations:** One of the key ways to do this is by making sure clear expectations are set at the beginning of every project. The best way I know how to do this is to post a set of "rules of engagement" for the team that clearly states the proper ways to interact, as well as what is expected from each team member. Some examples of these rules can include:

   - Each team member is expected to participate in any online discussions about tasks that they are involved in.
   - Each team member is expected to respond to direct communications From other team members within 24 hours.
   - Each team member is expected to complete the tasks they have agreed to or let other team members know about the changed situation.

3. **Doable Tasks:** Nothing can kill a team's morale quicker than burying them with a plethora of impossible tasks. Not everyone on a team is a Hercules (cleaning out the Aegean stables). It is best to begin with small tasks that provide the empowering experience of accomplishment for team members. It is important to acknowledge those triumphs. As noted in Rule 21, it is important to celebrate success to have continued collaboration.

Clear communication is critical to successful collaboration. In Rule 7 Stewart gives some more examples of how your behavior can overcome some of the challenges with virtual teams.

7 Structured Communications Support Successful Collaboration

When you begin any new project take the time to discuss the following ten elements.

Stewart Levine has a 20-year practice in helping people to communicate with each other better. He is a great practitioner of communication to support successful collaborations.

It is important to pay attention to formality and detail when building trust and setting expectations. This includes crafting clear agreements at the beginning of new collaborations, and having a process for getting back to agreement when conflict occurs.

In *The Book of Agreement* (Berrett-Koehler, 2003) I refined my template for beginning all collaborations. When you begin any new project, take the time to discuss the following ten elements. It will prevent a lot of conflict that erupts when people have different implicit expectations for the collaboration. You can create a template on a shared workspace. It is critical when working on projects with a new distributed team. I suggest you include the following:

- Intent and Vision: Big picture of what you want. Make it clear and specific.
- Roles: What is each person responsible for?
- Promises: What each person agrees to do and by when.
- Time and Value: The time the agreement will be effective. The value each person puts in and gets out, ensuring enough incentive for everyone.
- Metrics: Clear and measurable evidence you achieved your intention.

- Concerns and Fears: Challenges you are concerned about.
- Renegotiation: An understanding that it will become necessary to renegotiate because things change and everything cannot be anticipated.
- Consequences: For breaking promises, and the value lost if the project is not completed—for the individuals, the organization and society.
- Conflict Resolution: Agree to an "attitude of resolution," and an agreed resolution process when conflicts surface.
- Agreement: When you have discussed these issues ask whether you "trust" moving forward. Move forward only when you can say yes.

Here is an agreement one of my students worked out with a client:

- Intent and Vision: We will partner as a team to resolve this difficult situation. Your problem will be solved based on your values. We hold the end vision of you as a happy, satisfied client, and me as a fulfilled lawyer.
- Roles: You will be the client and co-collaborator, taking an active role in the process. I will be the wilderness guide, taking you through foreign territory.
- Promises: I promise to listen; understand what you want; be responsive to your needs and communications; confer with you at each choice point; remember it is your problem more than my case. You promise to—be available to strategize and answer questions; tell the truth; show up for appointments; pay fees on time.
- Time and Value: We will work until the matter is resolved. You will pay $2500, that will include up to 20 hours of service. If more time is needed we will come to a new fee arrangement. If the matter is resolved for $25,000 or less you will be satisfied with the value you received.
- Measurements of Satisfaction: Feeling of true partnership; client participation; timeliness of completion; effectiveness of communication; relationship with adversaries; sense of true resolution and completion.
- Concerns and Fears: I am concerned you will not collaborate and not make timely financial payments as requested. You are afraid I will not listen and that your problem will become my case.
- Renegotiation: It will be ongoing as the situation continues to change and develop.
- Consequences: You will not get the result you want and I will not get the satisfied client and the testimonial.
- Conflict Resolution: Use the method we learned from Stewart Levine.
- Agreement: We both believe we can collaborate effectively and be joint problem solvers.

8 Agree on a Process for Resolving Conflict

Look for a solution that addresses all concerns in the situation.

This is the third rule that Stewart contributed. This one focuses on the cycle of resolution in which Stewart goes through seven specific steps for resolving interpersonal conflicts.

Remember, no matter how good, your agreements are, disagreements and conflict will surface. The following steps will get you back on track and enable "Sustainable Collaboration." In my first book *Getting to Resolution: Turning Conflict Into Collaboration* (Berrett-Koehler, 1998) (second edition coming October 2009) I developed the following 7-Step Conversational Map for resolving conflicts. Here's an explanation of each step which really is less complex than it may appear at first glance and really has only three interactive steps—tell the story, deal with the emotion and create a new agreement.

The steps are:

1. Attitude of Resolution – A mindset I have come to call *Resolutionary Thinking*. Essentially it means, "Let's work this out!"

2. Telling Your Story – Getting the facts and listening to all stories. When you listen with a careful ear and honor everyone's story about a situation, you take a big step toward resolution.

3. Listening for a Preliminary Vision of Resolution – Look for a solution that addresses all concerns in the situation. Shift from the desire to win and get your way to a vision that everyone can buy into.

4. Dealing with the Emotion: Getting Current and Complete – When the situation is heated clearing the air by saying the things that often go unexpressed is essential. Drill down into what's not working, what's disappointing and whatever needs to be said. It is a way to face the good and bad in any situation, and let go of the disappointment of unrealized expectations.

5. Seeing a Vision for the Future: Agreement in Principle – A general understanding of the foundation of a new agreement, a broad brushstroke vision of the future.

6. Crafting the New Agreement: Making the Vision into Reality – A detailed vision of the new future.

7. Resolution: When Your Agreement Becomes Reality – With a new agreement you freely move forward, devoting your energy and intention to desired outcomes. You have a new sense of freedom because you have spoken everything that needs to be said, have completed the past and constructed a clear picture of the future and the map that will get you there.

I have used this model to resolve many hundreds of conflicts in virtual settings. These have included disputes between team members, partners, department heads, couples and employee disputes. Having the mental model of a roadmap provides a way into, through and out of a conflict. When you provide the right context and container, people respond well.

9 Communicate Frequently, but Briefly

Collaboration technologies need to be very low cost in time and effort, signal members' presence and availability, and be equally available to all members.

Eric Richert pioneered the creation and management of integrated (places, technologies and policies) work environments in support of new ways of working at Sun Microsystems, Inc. He formed 8 Corners Consulting in 2007.

Small, frequent doses of communication are critical to the health of collaborative teams, particularly teams chartered with creating innovative products and services with uncertain paths to success. Small, frequent doses of conversation assure good health characterized by timely coordination, open information and idea sharing, quick updates on decisions and changes, and knowledge of "what's going on" within the team and the larger organization.

When teams are physically collocated, informal conversations can be so tightly interwoven into people's workdays that they are hardly noticed.[4] We are apparently often unaware, in retrospect, of the brief, frequent interactions in our work teams, until they are missing.

That's what can happen when team members are physically distant from each other. Many teams grapple with what is lost—the water cooler, hallway and "over the panel" conversations—when groups are distributed or individuals are remote.

---

4. Sun Microsystems Open Work Surveys administered to multiple organizations inside and outside of Sun, 2002–2008.

This loss is not necessary. Some distributed teams do engage in frequent, brief, unplanned interactions (open source software developers appear particularly skilled with ongoing social and work-related banter). Generally, to do so requires: explicit team agreements; intentionally kick-starting the process of knowing each other; and technology that the entire team can use conveniently and easily.

The contrast between how co-located teams versus distributed teams achieve communications density is summarized in the following table:

	Formal Structure	+ Knowing Each Other	Requires	to Support
Collocated Groups	Policy of same place, same time work for all	Built over time through many routine interactions	Physical places plus degrees of technology	Informal communications and communication density
Distributed Groups	Group process, protocol, and technology agreements	Intentionally kick started and nurtured	Robust technology plus degrees of places	Informal communications and communication density

Explicit team agreements need to be established at the initiation of a project, or, for an ongoing work group, refreshed regularly. These agreements need to cover logistical protocols, key processes, and communications protocols.

Kick-starting the process of knowing each other allows teams to quickly know each member's role; what expertise, experience, and work style each brings; and each others' work context such as other work assignments or extraordinary family pressures.

Easy, convenient technology establishes the open channels needed for quick conversations. It needs to be very low cost in time and effort, signal members' presence and availability, and be equally available to all members.

10

Clear "Rules of Engagement" Support Successful Collaboration

A good example is to make sure you have clear and explicit written agreements detailing how a project will move forward.

Stewart has contributed more rules to this book than anyone else except me, and that is no surprise since he was my co-author for our last book (Collaboration 2.0). He and I have talked about "rules of engagement" for a long time, and I am glad he finally codified some of that wisdom into a rule.

In Rule 6 we looked at different best practices for clear communication for virtual and geographically distributed teams. In this rule we examine some additional behaviors to support successful virtual collaboration.

Formality of Process & Communication: When we work virtually it is important to develop, agree on and be more formal and deliberate about our communication processes. If you do not, things can get out of hand very quickly because you do not have immediate access to the receiving person's unfiltered responses. In the F2F world you can adjust to or push back against the communication, but it is much harder to do this successfully in a virtual interaction. A good example is making sure you have clear explicit written agreements detailing how a project will move forward. It is important to include such things as what each person will do, metrics for results, and how you will resolve the inevitable conflicts that will arise.

Think before you Speak: There are both synchronous and asynchronous collaborative interactions. For real-time interactions it is important to remember that you don't have to reply immediately. You can take a few seconds or a minute to respond. Just let the person you are interacting with know that you are doing this. Saying something like, *"Give me a minute, I need to think about some of the implications of what you have just said,"* is a good way to let the other person know what you are doing and that you are considering what they have said seriously, and not just ignoring them or focusing on your email.

For the asynchronous interactions there is good news and bad news about the buffer of time that these technologies support. The good news is the opportunity for sober reflection. The bad news is festering anger.

Checking in as a Way of Being: Since people are working at a distance it becomes essential to reach out and connect with others to make sure they remain engaged, committed, connected, motivated, and inspired. The manner of reaching out is your choice—but staying connected is essential to building a high performance team. Some of the high performance teams we have looked at:

- Have a weekly "issues" meeting to discuss any team problems that come up quickly before they have a chance to get worse. If the issue is critical to the project or the team, any team member has the right to call an "issues" meeting within 24 hours.

- Conduct an online survey or straw poll of all team members about a specific topic to understand what each of the team member thinks about the situation.

Take 100 percent Responsibility: Everyone on the team is responsible for results and everyone needs to take total responsibility for the project and its execution. It's easy to blame challenges on others when you are at a distance. Catch yourself! If you have ever worked in a start-up company it is not unusual for people to have multiple roles because there are too few people to cover every role needed. However, if you ask anyone in the start-up who is responsible for sales, they usually will point to the VP of Sales (if one has been hired) but say something like, "Everyone is responsible for sales."

Rule 19, the last rule by Stewart in this book, looks at creativity, measurement and training as critical aspects of conscious communication and successful collaboration.

11 Collaboration Technologies Magnify Your Message

Humans are emotional, electronic communications technology is not. Humans say things they do not mean, and mean things they do not say.

*Joy Gilfen is very passionate about collaboration and often blogs about it at JoyThinks.com. She is the author of **Flipping the Joy Switch, Inner-Outer Collaboration** and **Take Charge of Your Destiny**.*

"Which communication or collaboration technology should I use for...?" This is a question I get asked almost every day. My usual reply is, "Depends on your specific circumstances." But one thing I advise everyone on is to think about what type of message they are sending and carefully consider the content of the message.

When you use technology for personal or sensitive communications, it's wise to think first about the medium. Always review what you wrote before you press the send button, as there is no "take it back" button. Poorly thought through communications can get misdirected, broadcast in error, and multiply while taking on a life of their own. The ripple effects can cause hurt, create embarrassment, and cost time and lots of money to clean up. Be alert. Think first.

Today we Tweet, post, blog, email, text, post pictures...usually without thinking of the unseen consequences of our actions. The world is changing fast, the volume of communications decisions increases, and snap decisions are made. We get numb, and mistakes can multiply.

Professionals have written emails that have sparked investigations. Kids have posted pictures thinking they are communicating with their friends in a safe blogging environment, and suddenly they are being fired from a job, or stalked by someone they had no idea was reading their messages.

We used to share personal thoughts in private, and had time for reflection. Impacts were generally localized. We had time to correct.

Not today. Something happens, we react. Within a minute or two our reaction can be broadcast to thousands. Think first. Respond on purpose.

Understand the nature of your message: Are you sending an emotional or otherwise sensitive message? Maybe an electronic response is not so smart.

Humans are emotional, electronic communications technology is not. Humans say things they do not mean, and mean things they do not say. This matters in accurate communications. The medium is the transmitter of the message. If the medium cannot transmit the meaning fully, the full meaning can be lost or misconstrued.

Data that has no additional human context or meaning transmits fine. Data that needs *meaning and context* is different. If it is missing or inflammatory, it can get misused. So think first whether your medium, or transmitter, can contain the context and the meaning you intend to convey.

Consider the physical limitation of the method: When using written or verbal as opposed to in-person communication, we often lose 85 percent of our meaning. We lose the sensory, non-verbal, human part. So in personal or sensitive communications, text-based technologies limit the probability of accurate communication to under 15 percent forcing your reader to fill in the blanks with their own interpretation or speculation.

Consider the Permanency of the Communication: Will there be a record? Will your communication cause actions and decisions to be made? Angry emails can be saved, duplicate and transmitted to others.

Consider the ripple effect of being misunderstood: Collaboration technologies are a magnifier and can amplify gossip. In a Web 2.0 world a free blog (by the right person) can outweigh a $30 million dollar well-orchestrated advertising campaign.

12 Define the Problem Tightly

Because by tightly defining the problem, they were able to eliminate a lot of bad options that would have been generally good at collaboration, but not so good at solving their specific, most pressing needs.

Jason Pratt started his career as an architect, but right out of college he realized that the interesting action was in technology and the Internet. Because he has a deep love for architecture and the building industry, he decided to try and combine the two. This took him straight to industry leader Autodesk, where he worked in the collaboration division, eventually going on to be a co-founder of Buzzsaw.com, Inc., a collaboration site for the building industry.

People really don't want to collaborate. What they want to do at work is to **solve problems**. Sometimes problems are big and complex, and require more than one person to solve. In such cases people have to combine their efforts and skills and work on the problem together, and we call that collaboration. The goal of the collaboration is simple: **to solve the problem at hand**.

This insight may seem obvious, but it's fundamental to making good business decisions about collaboration. I've helped literally hundreds of companies large and small implement and use collaboration software since 1997, and I can tell you without question that the companies that improve collaboration successfully all share one trait: they are looking to solve a very specific, measurable business problem, and that's why they're looking at collaboration systems.

On the other hand, the companies that fail to implement successfully, or whose users stop using the system (or can't be made to use it in the first place), are generally the ones that felt like they needed "better collaboration" in a general sense, and went out and bought a system **without a specific goal in mind**. Here's an example:

I worked with a large construction contractor who set out to improve performance on a convention center project. Construction companies have large amounts of information to share with dozens of external partners and internal employees, and that information changes a lot. If a contractor is about to start a big project, they have to make sure all their suppliers and subcontractors have the right information about what to build. Documents shared on a big project include plans, specifications, scopes of work, change orders, submittals, daily reports, pay applications, work orders, requests for quotes, and a whole list of other documents that are used daily to track work.

The traditional way of collaborating involves lots of printed drawings, FedEx packages, coordination meetings, phone calls, emails, faxes, and so on.

The smart managers at this company prioritized the various components of their problem and got specific. They determined that just three types of documents (Plans, RFIs, and Change Orders) were responsible for the vast majority of problems on past projects. It isn't that those other documents aren't important; they just weren't as much of a problem for this company.

So, instead of defining the problem they're trying to solve as "sharing documents on the convention center job," they defined it as "sharing plans and tracking RFIs and Change Orders on the convention center job," which right away greatly improved their likelihood of success.

Why? Because by **tightly defining** the problem, they were able to eliminate a lot of bad options that would have been generally good at collaboration, but not so good at solving their specific, most pressing needs. Measuring the performance improvement in these tasks on the project will tell them whether their collaboration system is paying off as they anticipated.

Besides email and simple file sharing, very few collaboration tasks are generic in nature. Find out what the specific unique business problem is that your people are trying to solve, and implement a system to make that problem go away. You'll get immediate return on your investment, your people will be happier, and then you can move on to solving the next set of issues that your business faces.

13 Collaboration Starts with Understanding

Members of work teams collaborate with the belief that they're able to place an idea from their own mind cleanly in the minds of others, with clear understanding, through the use of words.

Rob Langejans, Haworth, Inc., believes that the assumption that we communicate clearly through the use of words is false. The definitions of words are found in dictionaries, but meanings are found in people. Increase your team's speed and accuracy by applying three steps that get to the meaning of important words.

Say you're leading a project team whose task is to implement a "Global Networking" solution for your organization. The first thing you do is organize a kickoff meeting with the team and bring in a consultant to offer some guidance. The meeting starts and the consultant goes into a training session on how to write an effective "elevator speech." You love it! It's perfect for getting the team and others to prepare to network (make key contacts, find new business) when traveling to other countries. The team is a little confused.

As you read this scenario, what was your interpretation of "Global Networking?" Is it possible that if we asked several people to define the team project they would offer different interpretations? Different understandings? And would each person even defend their own interpretation of what is meant by "Global Networking?"

Think about how often you communicate with your significant other, your kids or a good friend and have to explain things twice because the person you were speaking with didn't get it the first time. Frustrating, isn't it? You don't always know that they didn't get the point until they ask a question that surprises you in its simplicity—it's so clear in your mind...how can they not see it the same way?

Members of work teams collaborate with the belief that they're able to place an idea from their own mind cleanly in the mind of others, with clear understanding, through the use of words. This is a common assumption in any dialogue in and outside of work. Unfortunately, using words rarely conveys the meaning we hope for, and we don't even know it. A good friend may stop you during your story to clarify the meaning of a word you used, but when working collaboratively with others in a work setting members of the group might not be so bold as to interrupt, or be willing to admit that they don't understand. The problem goes beyond fear to the fact that we don't even know that misunderstanding is going on. And when collaborating with technology as the enabler, the situation worsens. For successful collaboration, get clear on the meaning of words. Teams require clear understanding.

The results of clear understanding are speed and accuracy. Let's take the word "collaborate"—a good place to start—does your work team have a common understanding of how the word applies to each member's contribution to the project scope? I promise you that in a group of four or more people, the term has different meanings. Having a common understanding (not definition, but understanding) from the beginning will speed up the results of the collective work being done. Moreover, the accuracy of the group's output will dramatically increase. Clear understanding of words will lead to speed and accuracy.

In his book, "Let's Get Real or Let's Not Play," Mahan Khalsa writes that when working with clients, we apply the motto: "No Guessing." For effective collaboration we need to agree on common terms first, and then agree on less common terms that are specific to the project at hand. Even more important is to agree on the meaning or application of the term for what we are trying to accomplish. Definitions are found in dictionaries; meanings are found in people.

14

Flexibility and Familiarity Are Critical for Successful Collaborative Communities

Make the community a focal point where members know they can get the best information first.

Tim Hughan is the Director of Marketing for Altus Learning Systems, a collaborative knowledge sharing solution that marries on-demand video and collaboration services to improve knowledge sharing, training and communications for geographically dispersed audiences.

Communities are a little like cocktail parties, you want to get the mix right so the conversation flows freely and everyone wants to come back for more. By inviting people with similar interests, the community will have a built in starting point to create conversation that branches naturally to related content areas.

Have a Plan – Create a community of focus so people know what they are supposed to be collaborating about and there is enough interest to build and maintain a vital community. Have some objectives and establish a team to create a baseline of content; documents, blogs, contributed links. Determine one or two objectives that most align with the main objective of the community.

Neatness Counts – Get your information design right. Make it as easy as possible for people to find and add content, but establish design guidelines and content suggestions to encourage quality of contributed content, not just quantity.

Feed the Beast – Add content, and then continually feed the community. Create a dynamic place where people find what they are looking for, are encouraged to participate and collaborate. Encourage users to create their own communities for them to take ownership of the site and take it into new areas of interest, but keep communities in line with original objectives. Reward experts for their knowledge and commitment.

Promote, Promote, Promote

Facebook, MySpace and LinkedIn did not spring from zero users to millions overnight. By establishing the benefits to users (Facebook – tell everyone about Me!) or LinkedIn (professional skills) and promoting their communities though informal formal channels, they were able to build their audiences. Promote your community through existing communications channels to grow your installed base of users and contributors.

What's in it for me? – Make sure the audience understands what is in it for them. Collaboration has been shown to have a positive effect on organizational productivity, but remember that individuals provide the content. Establish rewards for top contributors through ratings, featured content, and top 10 lists. Above all, keep the needs of the members first.

Plan a coming out party – Promote the community and its featured content wherever you can on existing content sites. Consume other collaboration efforts into your community and encourage new members to join.

Success as a self-fulfilling prophecy – Promote increased usage to encourage others to take a look to see what they are missing out on. Make the community a focal point where members know they can get the best information first. Get the most influential person in your organization to be a champion. Mention your community on every call, meetings, etc. as the source of information on a topic. Get people selling for you; work hard at customer service to get net promoters.

Use the Community

Put the latest, greatest information on the community site. Use the site for collaboration, break the email habit and fill out your profile, make a blog, and be **active**. Build cross-functional teams and encourage your team to model the behaviors you want to see in the community.

15 Make Someone Responsible for Collaboration

The appointment of a collaboration coordinator is a signal to the organization that collaboration is important and that the business is serious about enhancing its collaboration capability.

Shawn Callahan is the Founding Director of Anecdote Pty Ltd. Anecdote uses innovative storytelling (business narrative) and collaboration techniques to help large organizations redesign and improve the way people learn, share information and retain knowledge in an organization.

"Collaboration takes more than just wishful thinking."[5]

The trouble is, collaboration is a skill and set of practices we are rarely taught. It's something we learn on the job in a fairly hit-and-miss fashion. Some people are naturals but many of us are clueless. Establishing a collaboration capability requires someone to foster its development. People would think you are crazy if you suggested a company establish a sales capability without sales people or a human resources capability without an HR team. Yet, we have seen organizations wishing for a collaboration capability without identifying or resourcing people responsible for developing it. Wishful thinking is not enough.

To create a collaborative culture, you need to appoint someone with the experience to identify collaboration opportunities and bring them to life and to systematically build collaborative practices into the fabric of the organization. The

---

5. Callahan S., White N., and Schenk M., 2007, Building a Collaborative Workplace, [Online] Available at: http://tinyurl.com/459nk3
anecdote.com.au/whitepapers.php?wpid=15

coordinator is not an 'expert' in any particular specialization but is a person who is passionate about working with people, has a high credibility among peers, and is sociable.

"While engaging with stakeholders, one agency advised that while they could see some potential benefits in being part of this 'collaboration initiative,' they were simply too busy preparing to undertake a major six-month project (an IT upgrade). Recognizing an opportunity, the collaboration coordinator asked if it would be useful for agencies that already have some experience in planning and implementing this upgrade to give them advice (via a 'Peer Assist') on what they have learned about upgrading. The answer was a resounding 'Yes!' The coordinator put together and facilitated the event, ensuring that participants got high value for the time invested in the activity. Many valuable ideas, documents and software code segments were shared. The collaboration coordinator also gathered the material generated by the Peer Assist and loaded it to the knowledge base. The Peer Assist provided the participants with valuable benefits, generated new knowledge and artifacts and helped populate the knowledge base."

The role of the collaboration coordinator (evangelist, manager, specialist—the title doesn't really matter) would include:

- **Seeking opportunities:** finding situations in the organization where better collaboration would make a difference to the quality of products and services, the speed of delivering these products and services to clients, and the ability to use a diversity of ideas and approaches to innovate
- **Embed collaborative practices:** helping people learn and adopt collaboration practices and tools and keeping up-to-date with the field
- **Impact assessment:** collecting stories of how collaboration really works for the times you need to justify the role
- **Investing in relationships:** connecting people and ideas so new collaborations might flourish

Those organizations that move beyond wishful thinking and commit resources to establishing a collaboration coordination role can often face the frustrating dilemma of wanting the job done but being unable to free someone to do it. The appointment of a collaboration coordinator is a signal to the organization that collaboration is important and that the business is serious about enhancing its collaboration capability.

16

Foster a Culture of *True* Professional Candor

We often say what we think people want to hear rather than what they need to hear to keep the peace, avoid the challenge of managing another's disappointment or risk escalating the conversation.

William (Bill) Black, B.Sc. (QS), LEED AP National Director, Strategic Business Solutions, HAWORTH Inc. talks about professional candor in this rule, and encourages it for successful collaboration.

Candor (Noun): The initial definition is what you might expect—"the state or quality of being frank, open, and sincere in speech or expression."[6] That in itself is probably how most of us would understand and define candor in the context of collaboration. However the definition continues... *"freedom from bias; fairness; impartiality: to consider an issue, the ability to make judgments free from discrimination or dishonesty"* and *"the quality of being honest and straightforward in attitude and speech."*

Most people would assume that candor would actually be a prerequisite for collaboration, or a cornerstone of trust. But what we often consider to be candor is not necessarily the case. We permit outspokenness to masquerade as candor. Sometimes "frankness" masks the real agenda or can even be used to stifle other opinions or ideas. It is not that people are fundamentally

---

6. Dictionary.com, "Candor," in WordNet® 3.0. Source location: Princeton University. http://dictionary.reference.com/browse/Candor. Available: http://dictionary.reference.com. Accessed: January 07, 2009.

dishonest but candor is often sacrificed for the convenience of favor and harmony, even job security. For example:

- A hesitancy to be frank in case of causing offence or a negative response.
- Conversations afterwards in the corridor, water cooler or elsewhere where completely different (often contrary) opinions are expressed (too late to be of value in the real conversation of course).
- A fear of stating a contrary opinion lest it offend others or worse still risk one being fired or demoted.
- Sugar coating statements to soften the harsher realities.
- Candor cannot be viewed as a threat to the authority, ability or integrity of individuals but it often is.

We often say what we think people **want** to hear rather than what they **need** to hear to keep the peace, avoid the challenge of managing another's disappointment or risk escalating the conversation. However, if we are able to practice candor, it can often have great and unexpected outcomes. New discoveries, learning or revolutionary breakthroughs are often only reached through animated debate. No single person can ever hope to have all the answers; only a group of individuals linked by purpose (or goal) in a culture of true professional candor can ever hope to truly collaborate. And if they do there are often unexpected outcomes: accidental discoveries (serendipity), epiphanies or revelations occur because of the free flow of ideas driven by the candor of the participants.

Jack Welch in his successful book, "Winning..." notes that "Candor in business—or in any kind of organization—is a rare and wondrous thing. Rare because, as we have discovered during our travels over the past seven years, so few companies have it. Wondrous because when they do, everything just operates faster and better."[7]

No tools or technology for collaboration will succeed if this key behavior is overlooked. Candor is the cornerstone of **trust**. It is language of partners, friends and accomplices—and it is such as these that make the best collaborators. These are the people I want to be in the room with—these are my dream team.

---

7. http://www.welchway.com/Principles/Candor-(1).aspx

17

Celebrate, Celebrate!

Celebration is how we show respect for a job well done.

Leslie Yerkes is President of Catalyst Consulting Group, Inc., an organizational development and change management consulting firm based in Cleveland, Ohio.

Celebration may be the single most effective yet underutilized management tool there is to improve collaboration. Yet, for collaboration in the virtual world it's the tool most often overlooked entirely.

We know that people require praise and recognition. And that, second only to feedback, praise and recognition have the greatest influence on morale, performance, results, and motivation. We know that what gets recognized gets repeated, what gets celebrated becomes habit.

To be effective, celebration should be both immediate and ongoing. Celebration deferred to the end of the project is a wasted opportunity to generate higher performance at the moment and build a reservoir of additional energy for future endeavors. Immediate celebration connects people as team members and generates intrinsic, internal motivation. Celebration at the completion of a project recalls the high points and successes of the team and reminds all members of the fun they had along the way toward the successful completion of their collaboration.

What's so powerful about this simple strategy of celebration is, it doesn't have to cost money, or use additional time, or require special training.

Even as simple as celebration is, it can be elusive. Often we find ourselves issuing 'four pokes for every stroke.' It seems to be our nature to first see what's wrong or isn't working rather than what's right and is working. But people also crave recognition for their work. Celebration is how we show respect for a job well done.

So, how do we celebrate? To be effective, celebration must be more than simply something to do; celebration must be a way to *be*. To see if you're *being* a person who creates a climate of celebration, ask yourself these questions:

1. Do I capitalize on the spontaneous opportunities for recognition?

2. Am I open to giving praise as well as receiving it?

3. Do I participate in the celebration of good work and high standards?

4. Do I contribute to making the work environment, both real and virtual, a positive situation?

5. Do I share in the work load equitably?

6. Do I find new ways, both little and large, to celebrate our success?

When Art Ryan became CEO of Prudential, he needed to change the culture. So, he found exceptional Prudential folks from several different offices and created a collaborative committee called OPX. Their task was to create the message of this new culture and develop the system to spread it through all 60,000 employees. The collaboration was successful in changing the culture and creating a company for which people loved to work. Janine Omara, Director of Human Resources, Newark, says that success, which helped Prudential put half a trillion dollars under management in the last six years, was because "…everyone had a stake in each other's success. There wasn't a sense of competition between employees. We had the synergy of extending ourselves, and good intentions to each other. Whenever we did anything right, we celebrated our success and we shared the celebration."

Celebration is the universal need that transforms people and things every time it's applied. The more we celebrate our collaborations, the more fun the collaborations are. The more fun the collaboration, the more we enjoy the work and the more success we have. To ensure successful collaboration, celebrate!

18 Plan Critical Elements of Your Business

Collaboration does not just happen through osmosis.

Pat Lupica believes that while collaboration is creative in nature and often thrives better in an environment without supervision, it must be deliberate, carefully planned and financed. Perhaps, and most importantly, it must include the right mix of people with the right attitudes.

A person would be hard pressed to find a business book today that does not stress the importance of collaboration, but is it really new? In the 80's (USA) there was quality circles and Deming's PDCA to promote continuous process improvement; the 90's brought cross-functional teams, lean, and six-sigma; the headliner today is innovation through partnerships. Regardless of the latest terminology, idea generation and continuous improvement remain at the top of the list for achieving competitive advantage, yet mastering the collaborative process to make it happen eludes many companies; they know they need it, most can sell it, some can do it in the short term, but few can harness it as a matter of routine.

We now have to ask the question, "Why is achieving collaboration on a consistent basis such a challenge?" "I'd love to collaborate, as long as I can work alone."[8] This is not an

---

8. Ellen Lupton, July 2005,
http://tinyurl.com/dbpzm6
aiga.org/content.cfm/why-collaborate, accessed 1.3.09

uncommon sentiment toward collaboration. It sounds great in theory, but is difficult, and at times painful, in practice. Let's explore some reasons for the sentiment.

Game Theory (the analysis of group interaction) explains it in part. [Intelligent] people will act a certain way (make decisions) in an effort to achieve their own goals, which we already know can vary from one functional department to another, and can most certainly differ between trading partners. For many people, it's just easier to get the job done themselves, especially when deadlines are pressing and everyone is overloaded. Then there is the nightmare experience of working with the person who is viewed as a freeloader—we have all had one on the team at one point or another. Lastly, there is the notion that sharing information somehow diminishes recognition or worse, someone else might be recognized for your work.

So What's a Company To Do?

Rewards and punishments could be aligned with collaboration goals, but this cure has been avoided for decades; it appears that the cure is worse than the disease (lack of collaboration), and alone, this would not be the cure-all.

Maybe current employees just need to be sold on the idea. No doubt, people can be inspired in the short term, but how will they hold up when issues previously discussed start to surface?

Maybe a firm just needs to hire the right people. And what do those people look like? Companies spend thousands of dollars on personality tests and profiling in efforts to hire the right people. While this is important, it is not the smoking gun.

What is suggested is that collaboration be planned and *financed* like other critical elements of your business—collaboration does not just happen through osmosis. Ideas are not diffused across functional boundaries or across external borders without a carefully designed and financially supported adaptive framework to include technology, tools, on-going training, protocol of how people will work together, and most importantly a culture that continually reinforces and supports an adaptive framework. The new mantra today is "doing more with less and *fast*." Achieving collaboration has to be a deliberate, strategic, and a planned function of the business. What kind of collaborative environment do you have? How much thought and resources have been dedicated for its design and implementation? And lastly, what's in the annual budget to keep the adaptive framework alive and evolving?

Measure What You Collaborate About for the Most Effect

Another issue is resistance to technology. People don't like to look like failures, stupid or incompetent.

Measuring the success or failure of collaboration is one of the hardest things to do. Stewart Levine looks at what some of the metrics are to help drive collaboration.

Collaboration as a human behavior can be both complex and interactive and it is hard to develop metrics that measure collaboration attitudes, behaviors, and outcomes. Below are some options to look at different metrics that can be applied to drive collaboration.

Creativity and Flexibility Reigns: Given that the territory is new, there is no off the shelf manual that will tell people exactly what to do and what will work. You are limited only by your own creativity and thoughtfulness.

Metrics for both Process & Productivity: It is axiomatic that what can be measured can be changed. This also applies to collaborative behaviors. Every project needs to develop objective metrics for determining success in terms of desired outcome and in terms of the process used. The objective is to have measurable criteria to which you can say "yes or no" in terms of results achieved and efficacy of the process. For example some easily measured and objective metrics could be:

- You did tasks 1, 2, and 3 on time (yes or no).
- 33 percent of the time you were late on tasks you agreed to do (yes or no).
- Your manager signed off on all steps of this process /decision (yes or no).

Technology & Communication Training: Since you are working at a distance, people may be challenged by both the technology and communication skills. It's important for everyone to have the resources for the education and learning they need. In some research by David Coleman of Collaborative Strategies (my co-author on our last book "Collaboration 2.0") found that if the manager of a team had poor communication skills, the probability of that team being successful was greatly diminished and the chance of that team being a high performance team was zero.

The way he dealt with this situation at a large clothing manufacturer and retailer was to have the team manager go through a rigorous training in communications skills. Because the manager of this IT team was technically oriented, he was great at working with machines and computer programs, but not so good at working with people. Because of his technology skills, he was continually promoted until he was one of the youngest team managers in the company. But like the "Peter Principle" formulated by Laurence J. Peter, he had risen to his level of incompetence, and one of the best ways to improve team productivity was to help the manager gain new and much needed communication skills. Although this team was collocated, team productivity improved dramatically after two months.

Another issue is resistance to technology. People don't like to look stupid, incompetent, or like failures. One of the best ways to combat these feelings is to do a proactive program of training. Not only does this help people feel competent with the technology but they also feel empowered in their initial use of the technology and so will use it again. Training also overcomes many objections from resistant users, and it also helps them to see how using the technology can benefit them and their team(s).

Virtual collaboration requires that we make our communications about content take the place of the subconscious verbal and auditory cues we get when interacting with someone F2F. The best practices below show how being flexible and creative in your interactions, being able to measure some of the outcomes of the interactions, and providing adequate training both on the collaborative technologies and processes, can power your team to high performance.

20 Know the Objective Before Defining the Tools

Knowing the business objective of collaboration is about defining these details so that an organization's tools, like its real estate, software and technology, and organizational culture, are designed to enable such behavior.

Rachel Casanova is an architect. She called me out of the blue one day about a year ago, and we had a great conversation about collaboration and how it can affect the physical workplace. This rule is common wisdom in some architectural firms, but it is not a practice that many people stick to.

My job is to figure out how the physical workplace can support an organization's strategic objectives. To do so, I assess their business goals, people strategy, and organizational culture to define a supportive workspace.

Over the last 10 years, I have consistently heard business leaders say that a key initiative is to "increase collaboration within the organization." These leaders can define what increased collaboration will achieve—more creative products or services, more cross-selling opportunities, fewer errors, increased speed—but the challenge for most leaders is the ability to articulate what successful collaboration really means. Do they mean communication or collaboration? Who needs to interact? What phase of work requires collaboration? What information needs to be transferred? What are the right means of collaboration?

Knowing the business objective of collaboration is about defining these details so that an organization's tools, like its real estate, software and technology, and organizational culture, are designed to enable such behavior.

We were recently engaged by a TV media company that was preparing to relocate approximately 2,500 personnel and wanted to use this change as an opportunity to improve efficiencies in the organization. We interviewed 20 mid to senior level managers to understand their business objectives and gain an understanding of how they thought the physical environment could enable their work. The results of those interviews concentrated around the need for collaboration. However, it wasn't until we probed further that we understood the underlying intent:

- To encourage people to brainstorm and critique creative concepts throughout the development phase of a project.
- To enable employees to have a better idea of the resources, knowledge, and programming content that was available within the multifaceted organization.

Think about some of the following space solutions that address the first objective:

- Provide large, uninterrupted wall space where work in progress can be pinned up
- Create centralized, open meeting areas
- Provide dry erase and interactive electronic boards where ideas can be generated and documented for others to see
- Design interesting, flexible environments that encourage creative thought

On the other hand, the second goal could not be solved in the same way. Perhaps such a requirement might trigger some of the following solutions:

- Formal and informal training programs
- Rotational job positions
- Knowledge management applications
- Adjusted reward structures

The opportunity, therefore, to create successful collaboration is to ensure that the intent is well understood so that the right tools are made available.

21 Collaboration Requires Management and Leadership

If employees represent 80 percent of the cost of a knowledge-intensive organization and these employees spend 70–80 percent on different types of collaborative activities, this should be the focus of attention for business executives.

The motivation for this rule is the observation that most companies tend to address collaboration in a fragmented, ad hoc manner, despite the fact that many professionals today spend most of their time on collaborative activities. The rule has been written by Dr. Kjetil Kristensen to help companies understand why they should approach collaboration more systematically.

Collaboration processes are by nature complex, contextualized, dynamic, and unpredictable. Many companies have detailed descriptions of many types of processes, yet little is said explicitly about how employees, consultants and others should collaborate to achieve business objectives. Typical knowledge workers can spend up to 80 percent of their time on different types of collaborative activities or interactions[9] and for many knowledge-intensive businesses, more than 80 percent of the cost of doing business is attributable to labor (personnel) costs. Now, if employees represent 80 percent of the cost of a knowledge-intensive organization and these employees spend 70–80 percent on different types of collaborative activities, this should be the focus of attention for business executives.

---

9. Butler, P., Hall, T. W., Hanna, A. M., Mendonca, L., Auguste, B., Manyika, J., et al. (1997). A revolution in interaction. *McKinsey Quarterly* (1).

In essence, productivity improvement in knowledge work depends on several factors, where IT investment represents only a single dimension. This should be taken into account when launching collaboration improvement initiatives, as the way collaborative work is organized and facilitated affects the nature of interactions, and the ability of these interactions to support fundamental business processes.

Managing collaboration is more about promoting and enabling the benefits of collaboration than it is about managing the costs. The reason for this is that the benefits, if managed properly, outweigh the costs of collaboration by an order of magnitude. Collaboration is about making people achieve together what they cannot achieve alone[10] and it is about making people more productive at what they do. As the costs of collaboration (awareness, training, technology, service) in most cases represent only a fraction of the personnel cost of a trained professional, even a modest productivity increase for these professionals would more than offset what cost-oriented IT and HR departments would consider a substantial investment. Collaboration management can hence be described as the facilitation of high-performance processes and productive interactions, through the ongoing management of the benefits of improved collaboration, combined with systematically addressing the foundations and preconditions of productive collaboration.

Collaboration leadership, on the other hand, provides direction and guidance, is more process-oriented and is related to demonstrating the benefits of collaboration, motivating others to work in new, smart ways, and inspiring collaborators and others to use collaboration as a pathway to improved team effectiveness and productivity. Collaboration leadership can be described as the attitude, mindset, values, and behavior key personnel possess that enable them to engage themselves and others in productive interactions and make collaboration work.

It should be noted that command-and-control mechanisms and micromanagement of specific processes or interactions are neither productive nor desirable for the vast majority of users, and therefore unlikely to succeed. Collaboration management and leadership is therefore not about micromanaging the processes and activities taking place, but focuses instead on facilitating and fostering a constraint-free environment for any productive interaction that help the collaborators achieve business and project objectives.

---

10. Hansen, M. T., & Nohria, N. (2004). How to Build Competitive Advantage. *MIT Sloan Management Review, 46* (1), 22–30.

Section II
Process and Policy

The rules in Section 1 were mostly about people and their various behaviors as they affect online or virtual collaboration. A critical aspect of collaboration is to be able to have the interaction be part of a process like development of a new product or service. Embedding collaboration this way not only puts the interaction in context for those performing the process but it also allows people to value the interactions. In certain organizations some of the processes have been codified into policies. The rules in Section 2 talk about how collaboration affects processes and policies.

The organization of this section starts with the application of collaboration to the process of accountability and then looks at the tension between security and collaboration. The next few rules focus on projects and specific processes like collaboration in supply chain, followed by processes for collaborating with specific groups or generations. The section ends with a rule about the process of making collaboration a core value and part of leadership.

22 Accountability Is the Next Step in Collaboration

In today's complex business environment with SOX and HIPAA regulations and increasing government oversight, collaboration is critical, but accountability is even more critical.

Gabriel Blanc-Laine is VP of Sales and Marketing at Qtask and is very much involved in developing collaboration tools that support Web 2.0 principles of transparency and accountability. This next rule looks at how, even with good collaboration processes, things can go wrong.

You just spent two hours in a long drawn out meeting hammering out the details of a complex multi-year project. There were eight people in the meeting, and a few others on the project team that were not in attendance. The project manager ran the meeting and also took notes about who was to do what, and why. A week later you are still waiting to be assigned specific tasks for the project, and can see from the Gantt chart that the project manager has posted various milestones for the project.

Months go by. There are more meetings, you are assigned more tasks, but this is not the only project you are working on and not the highest priority, so those tasks don't always get done on time. The project is a year late in finishing and over budget but your company has released a new widget into a very competitive market. After a few months customers have started reporting that in certain circumstances the widget has blown up. Unfortunately the widget has hurt several people and there is now a class action law suit being initiated against your company.

The project team is called together and this time the meeting is chaired not by the Project Manager but by a corporate lawyer. He is asking questions like, "How did you decide to do this? Was this tested adequately? Who released the widget into production?" Unfortunately for your company, you do not have a complete project or collaboration record, and so it is hard to determine not only what happened and by whom, but who is accountable. If the lawyer can't figure out how the decisions were made (there is no record of project conversations and decisions) this law suit may bankrupt the company.

This type of distributed team collaboration happens on a daily basis. It is hard enough to work with team members in different cultures and on different continents, never mind documenting everything on a project that is late and over budget to begin with. The last thing anyone wants is more overhead from a new collaboration tool, and if asked to use such a tool many on the project team will resist. So in order to keep a complete record (documents, conversations, decisions, tasks, etc.) the collaboration tool has to do much of this behind the scenes and not require any additional work from the project team.

In today's complex business environment with SOX and HIPAA regulations and increasing government oversight, collaboration is critical, but accountability is even more critical. In order to provide a complete record it would mean that the underlying database for the collaborative tool would have to link everything to everything else and there can be no silos of data that are not connected, which are often found in today's project management tools. The ability to connect all information and people is called "Hyper Collaboration" in that this connection architecture is like a hypercube and often reflects the notion of hyperlinks first proposed by Ted Nelson in the early days of the Internet.

There are very few Web 2.0 products that support this level of accountability, but because of situations like the one outlined above this more traceable level of collaboration is becoming a requirement for doing business. One of the new tools in the hyper collaboration area is Qtask, which was designed with the idea of accountability in mind (it is hard to go back and make a tool accountable).

Accountability is critical for both transparency and trust within any team, and if done right, can also increase productivity and cut costs.

23 Security vs. Collaboration

When we interviewed people on the support team, they talked about how invaluable IM was in supporting people to do back channel chat when they were on the phone with a customer and needed help with the answer.

In many of my past consulting assignments I have run into CIOs or IT people who believe that it is either security or collaboration. In many cases their organization is required to have a high level of security (bank or intelligence agency), and the culture of security can often defeat collaboration, regardless of what collaborative tools are used.

In these days of hackers and viruses many organizations have not only a CIO but a CSO (Chief Security Officer). Often the first thing the security officer sees is the collaboration risk from the use of different collaboration solutions. Organizations that prize secrecy over transparency, and are often top-down, command and control hierarchies, often see collaboration as a threat.

In order to deal with supposed threat, some organizations have created policies forbidding people from using specific collaboration technologies (IM/chat, social networks, and connecting with others outside the firewall). It is true that all of these collaboration technologies do pose some threat to security, but I first want to test the original assumption of security. It is my belief that nothing is secure—if you lock it up, someone can find a way to unlock it. You can make it hard, and expensive (or both) to get to specific information, but you can't truly say it is secure.

Okay, so let's say you're willing to live with my definition of security, and don't want things to become more insecure because of the variety of collaborative tools used by your organization. That does not mean you want to close off the collaborative tools to use, as they do provide value to the organization, and often can be critical to its healthy functioning. This also seems to be the way most CIOs see Web 2.0 technologies. However, it does not have to be either security or collaboration—it can be both.

A high tech client we worked with in Silicon Valley had a presence on three continents, and offices on both the West and East Coasts of the U.S. Their HQ was on the West Coast and the support team was on the East Coast. When we interviewed people on the support team, they talked about how invaluable IM was in supporting people to do back channel chat when they were on the phone with a customer and needed help with the answer. They were mostly using Yahoo Messenger and occasionally AOL or MSN to do presence detection and also for the chat conversations. The new security officer was horrified to find out that they were talking about corporate issues over a public IM system that was not encrypted in any way. When we asked the support team about this they said, "Why bother?"—it was not critical information they were talking about, and the chance of someone being able to pick their IM out of the stream was minimal.

The security office was still not satisfied, so we had to come up with a compromise solution that worked for both parties. We ended up using an IM gateway which not only supported IM encryption, but also allowed corporate policy decisions around IM to be implemented as it could detect key words in a message and either let it go through or block it. This compromise ended up working for both sides—support was still able to use IM and the security officer had made IM more secure.

Today more collaboration tools, especially consumer-oriented tools like social networks, are more focused on transparency than security. As the NetGeners (those born after 1982) move into the workforce they are more used to the transparency of today than the security imposed by the Baby Boomers. The NetGeners are also more used to using collaborative technologies. This can be a challenge for some organizations today. A high-tech client of mine, that made really cool products, was still using an old IBM/Lotus Notes collaboration infrastructure. When its young new hires met with the CEO at a monthly lunch, quite often they complained that the collaboration infrastructure at work was not even as good as what they were used to on their personal computers using Facebook, Twitter and other tools. Because NetGeners are sensitive about their work environment, many recruits soon left to find a company with a more modern collaborative infrastructure, making talent management a real problem for my client.

24

Manage Collaboration Like a Project

We saved countless hours of potential rework and produced a great outcome by treating the whole effort like a project.

Jason Rothbart works at a collaboration software provider called GroupSwim. He works with customers and prospects every day learning how to improve their ability to collaborate and produce results.

For a collaborative effort (requires more than one person and has an end goal) to succeed, it is useful to treat it like a project. The "project" should have a goal(s), timeline, common tools, and roles. I'm not talking about creating a formal project plan, but some basic planning and organization at the front end of the collaborative effort is an excellent investment of time and potentially money.

Most collaboration is poorly managed or not at all. While there is a *huge* variation in the level of effort, number of people involved, etc., the things good project managers do are helpful no matter how big the project. Even when two people are collaborating on the smallest of projects, the likelihood of success hinges on very predictable things.

First, the collaborators should agree on deadlines and consider any interim milestones. Second, they should decide who is in charge or at least responsible for packaging the final deliverable. Or, they should at least give one person the responsibility for coordinating the work, even if they aren't "in charge." Third, if it isn't obvious, they should coordinate the tools or software they might use so they don't end up with incompatible work that they need to rework in order to consolidate. Finally, they should also agree on goals or what the end of the collaboration will achieve. Is it a document, or a decision, or a piece of art, or meeting up at a ballgame, or some combination of many things?

Let's review a recent example. I led a team where we needed to collaborate on a long, multi-part document as part of a sales effort. The content and data this document required did not exist, and it was both long and complicated. It required focus, creativity and discipline to get it done by the time we needed it.

The team comprised of five people in different parts of the company in different parts of the world, across time zones. We used an application called GroupSwim and its Wiki as the software solution for this effort. Two of us spent time mapping out the collaborative effort. We developed the following "plan":

- Set deadlines over the course of three days, which is how long we had
- Divided the document into separate sections
- Assigned primary authors to each section
- Created a Wiki page for each section of the document and added the questions each author needed to address
- Tracked people's progress with a central Wiki showing status and hand-offs
- Reviewed each section as people completed them
- Consolidated each section into one comprehensive document
- Performed final edits and cleaned up language, voice, grammar, etc.
- Formatted the document and then published

The process worked to perfection and yielded a high quality piece of work. It would have never worked without basic planning in the beginning to ensure everyone knew what to do, when to do it, and how to do it. We saved countless hours of potential rework and produced a great outcome by treating the whole effort like a project.

25 Collaboration Can Make Projects More Successful

If a project fails (is late, over budget, or does not meet a specific goal) it is easiest to blame it on the tool or technology you used because that is the most tangible.

Many studies show that the main reason projects fail is poor communication between the people on the project team. Most vendors of project management tools have not realized this and have focused on tracking and reporting instead of collaboration and execution.

Project tools were initially built for large linear projects and for the professionals managing those projects. However today, most people who manage projects are not professional project managers and many people have begun to realize that projects are often anything but linear. In addition, most project management (PM) tools do not support the interactions of people on the project team with either project objects (schedules, Gantt charts, presentations, diagrams, documents, etc.) or with other people.

If a project fails (is late, over budget, or does not meet a specific goal) it is easiest to blame it on the tool or technology you used because that is the most tangible. Projects do fail quite often: according to a 2004 Standish *Chaos* report on project management success and failure, this report found that "29 percent of projects succeeded, 18 percent failed and 53 percent were challenged"[11] (where the project does not provide the same value as a successful one).

---

11. http://tinyurl.com/4wpjun
softwaremag.com/L.cfm?doc=newsletter/2004-01-15/Standish

The initial tools created for these projects focused on the linear nature of the project and included support for such concepts as PERT charts, critical path management, and eventually WBS (work breakdown structures) which captured critical dependencies in the project. The problem is that PERT-based linear models for projects were developed for large-scale, one-time, non-routine projects like the building of the Polaris missile. But it is not the tool that should be blamed, but the behaviors and interactions of those doing the project.

How Do We Fix the Tools?

Obviously something is not working, and one of the avenues of attack is to look at the tools to see how they can be improved. Not by adding more features and functions (like in Microsoft Project) but rather by looking at the underlying assumptions of these tools to see where needs are not being met. I believe that a new class of PM tools is emerging, driven by a number of pressures:

- The social nature of projects, and the easy availability of social networking tools and more sophisticated collaboration technologies in the consumer space.
- Support for both linear and non-linear project planning and better tools for estimation (both time and resources). This allows project managers to deal with "wicked problems" which can be much more challenging.
- That the current PM methodology does not apply well to many projects it is being used for.
- Most people using PM tools today are neither trained nor have the time to be trained and are not professional project managers. This means that tools have to be easy to learn and use, inexpensive and easily accessible—not only to the project manager, but to their team which may be distributed across countries, and companies.

Newer PM tools integrate not only asynchronous collaboration technologies (VTS – virtual team space) to create a secure virtual project space, but they begin to integrate RTC (real time collaboration) functions to support more rapid interactions (IM/Chat, SMS, etc.) between project team members, and cut down overall task and project duration.

Collaboration in Supply Chains – Supply Chain Management 2.0

SCM 2.0 refers to the combination of processes, methodologies, tools and delivery options companies utilize for rapid results and the agility to manage change.

Sandy Vosk is an expert in Supply Chain Management, and a lifelong learner. In our joint efforts to see how Collaboration 2.0 technologies can be applied to supply chains, we have learned from each other.

Supply Chain Management (SCM)[12] encompasses each entity involved in the storage and transportation of raw materials, inventory associated with work-in-process (WIP) and finished goods from point of origin to point of consumption. At its core, Web 2.0 empowers users to generate content, connect people to each other and connect people to the content they are looking for. Supply Chain Management 2.0 (SCM 2.0) refers to the combination of processes, methodologies, tools, and delivery options companies utilize for rapid results and the agility to manage change. The latter is of great importance due to the impact of globalization, drastic swings in oil prices, shorter product life cycles, scarcity of talent and the complexities of near/far and offshoring.

As in all business, human nature and organizational realities can get in the way of success. A collaborative relationship must be based on trust and strong leadership. Companies still struggle with poor communication across departments.

---

12. http://tinyurl.com/2elsve
en.wikipedia.org/wiki/Supply_chain_management

Supply chain collaboration requires changes in corporate culture, organizational structure and key business processes.

SCM 2.0 can provide substantial benefits in the order to cash process (customer collaboration) and the purchase to pay process (supplier collaboration). The supply chain processes where significant value can be gained include: customer service, procurement, manufacturing flow, distribution, outsourcing/partnerships, performance metrics.

Effective collaboration with suppliers and customers can increase customer satisfaction and create compelling results, such as:

- Administrative savings
  - Lower transaction costs
  - Fewer data errors (invoice discrepancies)
- Improvements in key performance metrics
  - Reduced out of stocks at customer/retail location
  - Increase in perfect order percentage
  - Reduced inventory holding costs/lower safety stock requirements
  - Faster order to cash cycle time

Cisco utilizes a collaborative planning strategy with cable and telecom customers to see as early as possible what large projects are coming that will impact the demand for these complex products. According to Angel L. Mendez, Senior Vice President of Global Supply Chain Management...we have seen dramatic improvements in delivery performance. By dramatic I mean, a shift from 65 percent on-time delivery to service levels in the high 90's."[13]

Cisco also utilizes a collaborative network to automatically monitor and control the quality and configuration of production and test equipment in 20 global partners' factories. The "Autotest" network has helped Cisco raise their quality standards because they can now identify problems in real time and quickly react to anything that is outside their Six Sigma limits.

Regardless of where you and your companies fit in the supply chain, effective collaboration within and between companies is a key differentiator for surviving and thriving in our global economy. Technology is an important factor and will continue to evolve but ultimate success will continue to be based on the quality of the relationships, agreements and communication between people.

---

13. "Collaboration Helps Cisco Systems Fight Growing Complexity" SupplyChainBrain.com, April 24, 2008

27

Collaborate Successfully Between Generations

A lot has been written about this first generation to grow up digital. Supposedly they have the ability to juggle multiple IM/chat screens while talking on their mobiles and listening to music.

You have probably seen your children (the current computer experts in the house) chatting with friends all over the world on Yahoo or AIM. They have a Facebook and MySpace page which you are probably afraid to look at, and you pray they did not put anything damaging online. Your generation would never do that!

I have observed how different generations use and extend trust (and ultimately collaboration) on the Internet. Below I have tried to summarize these observations to help you in your inter-generational interactions. Please realize that the way I characterize each generation is a generalization, and that not all people in that generation may act this way.

The WWII Generation/Seniors: these people are in their 70's and 80's now (my parents' generation), they lived through a World War (and possibly the Depression), they tend to be frugal and not very trusting. Online this generation also does not extend trust easily and are suspicious of anyone approaching them. If you are part of their generation and can share some context and history with them, or have a reference from a common friend or acquaintance that will help in their initially extending trust. However, once trust is extended you are in, and friends for life. The other characteristic of Seniors is to focus on secrecy rather than transparency. "Loose lips sink ships" may be a good phrase to characterize this generation. They don't believe that conflict, of any kind should be dealt with in a public forum, but are better dealt with one-to-one (usually by email or phone), and not as part of an online community or social network.

Baby Boomers: Okay, I admit to being one, but not always acting like one. Boomers are more familiar with computers, but are the first generation to deal with the conversion of communication and interactions from analog (paper) to digital (email) and so tend to use the paper analogs (email) more than other generations. However, they also seem to adopt new technologies much faster than the Seniors, and I find them in many different social networks and online communities. They are more willing to initially extend trust to people in their networks, and often will "Google" someone to find out about them if there is not much information in their profile. Since they used BBS (bulletin board systems) in the 80's they are more used to public discussion and forums, and are willing to deal with some kinds of conflict in a more public way.

GenX: These are the 30–40 year olds. They mostly grew up with computers and are comfortable with them. They are big into social networks and online communities, and are often a majority of the participants (in that they have enough life and work experience to have some level of expertise and have something to say) in these communities. This is the first generation that was not willing to deal with email and tended to migrate more towards real-time interactions. They are big on IM (chat/instant messaging) and SMS (texting) as well as web conferencing instead of face-to-face (F2F) meetings. As a matter of fact I have seen people of this generation sit in an F2F meeting and interact with others in the room via their computer.

NetGeners: A lot has been written about this first generation to grow up digital. Supposedly they have the ability to juggle multiple IM/chat screens while talking on their mobile and listening to music. They also are used to extending trust (and collaboration) online, and live their lives much more transparently than other generations. They not only are willing to do this but expect it from others no matter what generation. They also expect others to be willing to discuss most anything (even conflict) openly and as part of the community or social network. I have often seen NetGeners in conflict put the question to the group and ask for their advice or help with a decision. This is the Twitter generation, the micro-bloggers, willing to let their peers know where they are (location based applications) and what they are doing. They are defined by what online groups they are in and who they know and interact with. It is common for NetGeners to have a group of friends whom they talk with on a daily basis, who may be geographically all over the world, and whom they have never met in person.

28 | Collaborate with Mobile Professionals

They could also be anyone who spends their time in meetings, managing others, or working on teams or projects.

What technologies meet the needs of those who are always on the go, want to connect and interact from anywhere and have little patience for technologies that are difficult or don't work all the time?

Most collaboration technologies today are aimed at either the consumer or the enterprise. However, there is another population, quite a large one, called the mobile professional which is not directly served by many collaboration technologies. Although mobile professionals have not had collaboration tools specifically built for them, collaboration is their life blood. A larger and larger segment of this population is made up of NetGeners (born in the 80's) as they move into the workforce.

Defining Mobile Professionals

So what roles might mobile professionals play? They could be sales and/or marketing people or business development professionals; just as often, they are entrepreneurs, CEOs, or other "C" level executives. They could be PR or marketing communications people or consultants, or they could be in professions like medicine or law. They could also be anyone who spends their time in meetings, managing others, or working on teams or projects. In essence, a mobile professional could be anyone who collaborates with anyone else.

So what are the characteristics and work styles of mobile professionals?

- They tend to be geographically distributed.
- They tend to be driven individuals and are often entrepreneurial.
- They spend a good portion of their time working alone.
- They work in cross-functional groups and on high-performance teams.
- Their work requires them to interact fluidly both in real-time and asynchronously.
- They are willing to extend trust (and collaboration) to those they know (or sometimes to those referred to them through a social network).
- They work with a wide variety of content objects and media (audio, video, data, pictures, etc.).
- They tend to be impatient and don't want to spend time uploading documents or pictures, or learning new applications, or new functions.
- They are multi-taskers, and may have several applications open at once on their desktop.
- They expect to be able to detect the presence of others in their network (no matter what device they are on or where they are geographically).
- They expect to have easy and immediate access to data and content critical to the processes and tasks they are trying to complete.
- They are often found in coffee shops working away with their laptops and cell phones (often called Urban Nomads) oblivious to the chaos swirling around them.

What types of technologies are available today for these individuals. The first type of tool falls into the asynchronous collaboration area called Virtual Team Spaces (VTS); these tools help distributed teams store and share documents securely, and are often used by small teams (2–8 people) for projects. These tools can be both premise-based or SaaS (Software as a Service). Some examples of VTS tools are: PBWiki, Huddle, BaseCamp, and SharePoint.

A second type of tool is a real-time or synchronous tool. The most common example of this capability is either IM/chat or web conferencing. Some of the better known web conferencing tools include: LiveMeeting from Microsoft, SameTime from IBM/Lotus, WebEx (Cisco), Adobe Connect Professional, and GoToMeeting from Citrix.

29 Use Leaders as Collaborative Strategists

Optimum learning and development occur in systems where there is a rich web of interactions—this is collaboration.

Sheryl Sever, founder of Cross Currents Communications, believes that collaboration is a social imperative. Get the right people on the bus and in the right seats, with a commitment to building a best-in-class collaborative culture. Focus on internal-facing collaboration that encourages collective intelligence (simple yet intentional engagement), and recognizes those within the organization who consistently share information, resources, responsibilities, while engaged in and committed to organizational and personal excellence.

So, how do we as leaders create a culture that values, practices, and rewards collaboration?

Start with Talent Management

- Get the right people on the bus. Build a superior team by recruiting those who have a track record of working and playing well with others, and communicating with transparency, while confronting brutal facts.

- Make collaboration a core competency for any position. Define the specific functions and expectations in the professional development plan. Reward accordingly.

- Create a Collaboration Manager/ Coordinator position to promote, coordinate and manage your internal systems for knowledge sharing, skill and learning development. Look beyond HR, Marketing or Corporate Commu-nications for this collaboration evangelist. Design the position around com-petencies and overarching organizational goals and objectives.

Engage all your people in "big picture" solutions. Interestingly enough, a 2008 study available through the Society of Organizational Learning[14] shows that fewer than 35 percent of employees from 100 companies surveyed, know or are clear about how their role fits into the bigger picture—the overall business objectives and strategic plan. Best leaders motivate with questions, not initiatives.

When collaboration is a core value, employees are able to see the results of their work and the impact it has on company, clients, and col-leagues. This in and of itself is the reward.

Focus on "internal facing" online communities. Awareness Networks[15] released their 2008 white paper, revealing that 82 percent of over 162 leaders surveyed have seen that Web 2.0 technologies (particularly "company branded" Wikis) increase knowledge sharing, employee collaboration, and improved internal communications, and help employees "find" each other.

Continue to make Learning & Development a top priority. Optimum learning and development occur in systems where there is a rich web of interactions—and this is collaboration. As organizational leaders, ask where collaborative learning communities could be built or expanded upon. What new leadership and communication skills are needed cross-functionally to allow for full collaborative engagement?[16]

---

14. Society for Organizational Learning
(http://www.solonline.org/PublicationsAndResources/SoLNewsletter/)
15. Enterprise Social Media: Trends and Best Practices in Adopting Web 2.0 in 2008, white paper published by Awareness Social Media Marketing
16. Some of the more exemplary and evolving corporate university curric-ula that I have recently reviewed include: Disney, Cisco, Toyota, Joir de Vivre (the Mojo to Maslow approach). Adminstaff offers more than 3000 blended learning courses to their small business clients. MindJet has recently launched both an inward and external facing social community, featuring their own application that combines the best of social media, learning, and strategic visioning. Some of the most impressive learning communities have been birthed in the non-profit sector. Paul Hawken's WiserEarth.org site encompasses shared knowledge and learning commu-nities from more than 13,000 organizations worldwide.

Section III
Technology

I thought this would be the largest section of the book since I know so many people who either make, use, or focus on collaboration technologies. However, I have found technology to be an enabler of interactions between **people**. *Because technology is the most tangible, it is often what is focused on (or blamed if things go wrong). I found that only about 20 percent of the time was technology the culprit. The rules in this last section can help you choose a collaboration technology along with some of the best practices for using these technologies.*

The way this section is organized is that the rules focused on all collaboration technologies in general are grouped first, followed by subsections looking at rules for some of the simpler collaboration technologies like blogging and micro-blogging. The rules that follow build up to more sophisticated collaboration technologies like web conferencing and video conferencing and finally ending with a rule about collaboration in virtual worlds.

30 Focus on People and Process First

I saw this as a collaboration problem, but the sales manager saw it as a sales proposal problem.

For the last 20 years, I have been asked the question, "What technology should I use?" That is like asking a doctor what pill to take, without his even having the chance to examine you. Collaboration technologies are not a silver bullet, but a magnifier: if things are good it can make them better, but if they are bad these technologies can often make things worse.

Technology is the most tangible and visible part of electronic collaboration (computer-mediated collaboration). Weather it is a SaaS (Software as a Service) and part of "cloud computing" or traditional licensed software, the technology is the focus of about 80 percent of the conversations I have with people who are trying to figure out how to be successful with collaboration. The other 20 percent of the time, I get to talk with them about people and process. But this is completely opposite to what it should be. It should be 80 percent of the time, energy and attention go into the people and process issues rather than the technology, because 80 percent of the time, this is where the problems crop up (and only 20 percent of the time with technology).

I am aware that without the technology, we would not even be having these discussions nor would I be writing this book. I am not saying to ignore technology, but rather understand what your problems and pain points are around collaboration, and then pick a technology once you have defined your problem, the population it affects, and a plan for solving the problem.

For example: I interviewed a sales manager last summer. He complained that his company was losing more proposals than normal. I asked him how many proposals they wrote a month, and how many they expected to win. He said that they did about 10 proposals a month, and expected to win four or five, but lately (over the last few months) they had been winning only two or three proposals each month. Furthermore, the average amount paid on each proposal they won was $0.5 million, so losing two proposals a month was costing the sales manger about $12 million a year in revenue (that is a lot of pain!). I asked him what he thought the reason(s) were for this decline in wins. He said that it was hard to find experts (both within the company and in their supply chain and value network) to help work on specific sections of the proposal, and that teams working on the proposals were often late in getting them in to the client.

I saw this as a collaboration problem, but the sales manager saw it as a sales proposal problem. If I had offered him "sales proposal software" that would have alleviated his pain, he probably would have bought it, even if it did cost almost a million dollars. However, because this was a collaboration problem, I asked the sales manager to look at the process by which proposals were done in his organization. The process was anything but efficient, so we first worked on streamlining the process. We created templates for proposals based on winning proposals from the past. We interviewed employees at all levels and found that everyone was frustrated with expertise location, and outside of their personal networks, they did not know anymore who worked at the company, and what their expertise was. This was solved by applying an online community tool which not only had people create extensive profiles, but also linked keywords, and any work product (emails, online discussions, documents, pictures, etc.) they had done to their profile (with their permission of course) to make expertise location easier. Of course solving this problem for the sales manager means we have to solve it for the whole enterprise, which can be a daunting task, but take a look at Rule 18 which talks about the best strategies for successfully rolling out collaboration technologies to a large organization.

31 Collaboration Tools Should Be Easy

Collaboration is inherently complex as you have N^x relationships, where X is the number of people you are relating to. So making the collaboration tool complex just adds to the problem.

My motto is, "If a collaboration tool gets in the way or impedes the flow of conversation then it is not a good tool." In general this means these tools need to be easy to use and intuitive, otherwise they will not get used and often just sit on the shelf.

When I first started using collaboration tools (then called "groupware") about 20 years ago, there was no Internet, and these were generally desktop tools. They were often complex client-server applications (like Lotus Notes, which was released in 1989) that required IT professionals to support the application for the enterprise. Later Microsoft jumped into the fray with Exchange (which is even more complex than Notes in terms of servers and CALs licenses required). There were not 1200 collaboration tools available at that time, only a few, and they were often arcane and asynchronous tools.

When the Internet met the visual browser in 1995 everything changed and started to become "webified" and collaboration was no exception. Many applications still stayed on the desktop, but offered a browser-based interface. The next stage in the evolution of collaborative tools was the "web native" applications, which were built specifically using the browser as the client, and many tools did not require any download to the desktop. The current stage in this evolution is the movement of licensed collaboration tools into subscription services to fit with the trend in "cloud computing."

Being browser-based, some of these tools are both more intuitive (require little or no training) and easy to use. I talked about the "Mom Test" in the introduction as a way for me to determine how difficult collaboration software is. Most of the collaboration tools I looked at did not pass the Mom Test. However, we are in the new age of "cloud computing" where about half of all collaboration tools are now offered as a service (SaaS) often called "Software as a Service." There are some real advantages to a collaboration SaaS:

- Much lower start-up costs.
- You don't have to buy hardware servers to support the application.
- Because SaaS are mostly by monthly subscription, the software cost can often be listed as an operating expense rather than a capital expense (which are often much harder to get by management).
- You don't have to worry about hiring a person with specific technical experience to install, run and maintain a collaborative application; this is all done for you by the SaaS vendor.
- If security is an issue, or regulatory restrictions require you to have the software behind your firewall, you can choose an intermediate path (not a SaaS nor traditional licensed software) and some companies offer a "managed service" i.e., their software on your hardware behind the firewall, but they manage the application.
- SaaS is always up to date—no maintenance, no updating versions or rolling out a new version to the masses. The online version is always the latest, and a SaaS often will add features incrementally, without waiting for a version release like licensed software does.

Collaboration is inherently complex as you have N^x relationships, where X is the number of people you are relating to. So making the collaboration tool complex just adds to the problem. Many of the collaboration tools I have worked with suffer from "featuritis," the belief often ascribed to by engineers that putting more features into the tool makes it better. Actually, primary research we did for a client two years ago showed that the most popular feature (by far) in a collaboration tool was "ease of use."

In working with one of my clients, a collaboration software start-up we developed a definition of "easy" was "one or two clicks to do anything." An other feature that is useful is the fluidity of presence. People move back and forth between working alone and working with others throughout the day, but most collaborative tools don't support this. Good collaboration tools do not require you to change your behavior to accommodate the limitations of the software. For a collaboration tool, it must be easy, and the tool should not get in the way of the interaction, unfortunately today many commercial collaboration tools not only get in the way of the interaction but are the focus of the interaction because of technology issues.

32

Create the Ideal Collaborative Environment

Technology can actually help to break down barriers because it levels the playing field and in some way hides attributes which could lead to superficial judgments.

Audrey Scarff is a freelance consultant with expertise in web, intranet, and online collaboration. She has helped hundreds of clients achieve their internal communication goals through solid online strategies backed up by the functionality provided by Intranet DASHBOARD.

Encourage Trust and Participation

What works in a face-to-face environment is quite different from what we find when we take those conversations online. We lose the clues to what people are thinking, how they're reacting and other social cues. How can we create better feedback and trust within the team to encourage meaningful collaboration? Examples include:

- Video web-conferencing (visual cues)
- Smileys (emotion indicators)
- Facilitators/Moderators (people)
- Presence indicators (Who am I collaborating with? People know I'm here so I better contribute!)
- Profiles of team members to learn who they are, what their expertise is
- Learning the corporate language[17] and an acronym manager for Internet/chat slang[18]

---

17. Crowther G, 2003, 'CEO Communication – If you want them to listen, speak their language,' Communication World – The International Association of Business Communicators, Oct–Nov edition, p.34.
18. http://www.computerhope.com/jargon/l/lol.htm

Synchronous communications (where you are all in the same virtual room at the same time, such as live chat) can be a great tool during a project meeting where you need to have a quick side conversation.

Compare that with asynchronous communication tools (examples being online forums, bulletin boards, Wiki and blog comments) where the time between misinterpreting a message can be longer. Asynchronous collaboration is ideal for teams who aren't in the same place at the same time, and where people need more time to consider their response (especially in multilingual situations), and for grassroots collaboration.

Hint: In an asynchronous scenario, make sure the technology allows people to receive notifications to new contributions/posts (and know how to subscribe to them via RSS or email).

Remove the Barriers To Participation

In my experience some common barriers to participation include:

- Timing – when new participants join the group or conversation.
- Personality – shy, lacking confidence, loud, dominating.
- Language and culture.
- Technology interface – how easy is it to use?
- Lack of timely responses to contributions.

The first problem can be dealt with by having a formalized. Newcomers may be hesitant to contribute because they perceive the "onboarding process" group as too knowledgeable on the subject or history of the project, don't know who they're dealing with, or because of infavoidance[19]—they don't want to be seen to be asking a 'dumb question'.

Technology can actually help to break down barriers because it levels the playing field and in some way hides attributes which could lead to superficial judgments. It also enables shy people to contribute where they might otherwise not.

Most importantly having a good facilitator or leader helps to shape interactions and ensure all communications are acknowledged and answered. Finally you need to measure how well the collaboration is doing. This can be done by: number of posts, colleague ratings, cycle time improvement and ROI calculation.

---

19. Furnham A & Taylor J (2004), The Dark Side of Behaviour at Work, Basingstoke, UK, Palgrave Macmillan, p.29.

33 Change Management Ensures Collaboration

The developer or QA engineer who submitted his or her progress report online was exempted from attending the weekly status meeting.

Vadim Katcherovski is the founder and CEO of Logic Software Inc. which makes easyprojects.net. He has been in the software business for a surprisingly long time for a man of his age. In this rule he does not focus on the technology as one would expect, but on how the technology affects people.

People do not like change. Actually people hate change. Any new piece of technology you introduce most likely will be initially rejected or sabotaged unless people see a personal benefit.

And they will be right, because in most cases the new technology means confusion, added work or both. Think of Microsoft Office 2007. It is a brilliant application. However if you used a previous version of this product, then I can guess your first post-upgrade question: "Where the heck are all my menus?"

If you are in charge of introducing a new technology, especially a collaboration technology, you need to address this internal resistance and ensure a buy-in from the majority of your team members. This is generally called "change management" and below are some best practices that have helped me in these situations:

Don't Force the New System on Anyone

Never, ever just show up with a new tool and say: "Okay team, start using this software now."

- First, educate your team before introducing the new technology. Hold a short meeting and provide a brief overview of the solution. Explain the tool's importance to the company and why they are being asked to use it.
- Next, set up a pilot project and choose a core team of 4–5 people to participate. They are going to be your special task force driving the adoption across the rest of the organization.
- Make sure that all users have some basic training before allowing them to use the application on their own.
- During the trial period, meet with users and get their feedback.
- If some users were unable to evaluate the tool properly in the time allotted, try to persuade your vendor to provide additional trial time.

Show the Personal Payback

You will need to demonstrate people what is in it for them and how they will benefit personally from using the new technology. A friend of mine who is a manager in a software company told me this story.

The company's executive team was frustrated because of the lack of communication between the development team and the QA department. So, they decided to introduce new project management software to allow all team members to report their progress and track the efforts of all departments. But nobody used the program. When asked why, people complained that they already had too much on their plates. They saw it as a major nuisance and added hassle.

In response, the CTO of that company issued a memo. Any developer or QA engineer who submitted a progress report online was exempted from attending the weekly status meeting. The result was overwhelming. The next day virtually everyone posted their progress.

Make It a Habit for Everyone

When you have resolved all the issues and fully implemented the system, indicate to everyone the type of metrics or data you want to collect and make that input mandatory. You will need to check it regularly. If it is important enough to occupy your people's time, it is important enough for your follow-up, and is important enough to also be an indicator of change. Do not make exceptions for anybody. Do not accept excuses for failure to use the tool. Its use must become routine—a very useful habit.

34 Communication Improves with Collaboration Technologies

But don't expect software alone to be the magic bullet that keeps your projects on target. Human involvement will clearly determine the success of any project.

AJ Wacaser is the founder and CEO of PlanDone, Inc., a Web-based project collaboration services company serving small to medium-sized businesses. Growing tired of missing deadlines and incomplete projects, AJ developed PlanDone to help companies complete their projects on time.

We all know the benefits of collaborating on projects using technology, but are we asking too much of the technology? Can the technology realistically replace or improve on the face-to-face interaction of a traditional meeting? Once you get together and collaborate—what are the next steps for all involved? From a corporate bottom-line perspective, does the ROI end justify the means?

Many times data are not captured or misinterpreted without getting clarification, and technological solutions compound the problems by documenting it online. The old saying holds true: 'Garbage in; garbage out.' Staff in remote, outsourced locations often feel left out, ignored and "out of the loop." Too often the collaboration technology is more trouble than it's worth and will generate productivity losses greater than the actual cost of the product.

Some of the Benefits

Project management (PM) technology can literally transform the way you manage projects. But it really requires a new way of thinking and better communication. How can technology actually improve communication? One way is by holding all users accountable (see Rule 22).

Software technology can show the status of projects and where bottlenecks are. Acting on this depends more upon the people and the environment in which the work is being performed.

Case in Point

A project manager was convinced he had a rock star employee and justified his high salary with glowing reports to board members. Just one problem—the manager had no way to prove the success of this employee until he began using collaboration software. The project manager and the entire team soon discovered the employee didn't live up to the hype, and he was fired. He took credit for other people's work when it benefited him.

But don't expect software alone to be the magic bullet that keeps your projects on target. Human involvement will clearly determine the success of any project. Teams get credit for who they are, and what they do, not the product they use. The software should support the people and not vice versa.

Create a Communications Plan

Creating a communications plan is essential in managing projects. This plan must clearly define the process and the timing of the project to all involved. Your plan should keep all recipients or stakeholders updated on the progress of the project—goals, resources, status reports, budgets, etc.—in a timely manner.

An effective communication plan can make the difference between success and failure of your project. If you're searching for project management software to help you with your projects, consider one that allows you to communicate clearly and easily with your team, as well as one that provides reports for status updates.

35 Applying Collaborative Principles to Transactions

Integrate collaboration and transactions wherever possible.

John Tibbetts is a software architect and active developer. For the past 21 years, through his consulting company Kinexis, he has helped enterprises and vendors improve efficiency and increase reuse by implementing coherent software architectures for their applications and products.

Collaborative technology has immeasurably improved communication, knowledge-conservation, and skill utilization in the enterprise. So it's beyond ironic that probably the key enterprise task—processing transactions—remains a largely collaboration-free zone. The technology that has evolved to record business decisions via updates to the enterprise database has neglected the fact that decisions have to get made and they are made by people. My rule is that we should incorporate this collaboration phase into our transactional applications.

Transaction-processing is a discipline that dates from mainframe days. It ensures that updates to the database are complete, accurate, and irreversible. It requires a single user at a fixed location to engage in a real-time, highly formalized interaction with the transaction-processing software. If anything unanticipated happens, or if the user takes too long, the transaction aborts and everything must start over. This process reflects the way that computers work and has almost nothing to do with human activity.

Transactional software wants work that is complete, error-free, and ready right now. But, obviously, many transactions only get complete and error-free over time. Input from multiple departments might be required. Somebody may have to do some research. There may be discussion and negotiation. Estimates may get firmed up and rough proposals refined. And then there is the review and sign-off process.

This entire collaboration, alas, frequently takes place "out of channel," completely disconnected from the application that will evaluate and process the transaction. To a startling extent, people working on business transactions still rely on phone calls, emails, and conversations around the microwave. Only when the decisions have been made and agreed to does someone open the actual application and record the results. It's like collaborating on a document that can't be typed into a word processing program until it has been perfected on paper.

This is inefficient and risky. Potentially high-stakes business deals are under discussion, and the discussion is literally off the record. The result is that decisions are essentially anonymous. The process cannot be reconstructed. Identifying where a piece of data came from, or who changed it and at what point, is impossible. If you want to go back and extract some metrics about the decision-making process, forget it.

Our rule is to try to integrate collaboration and transactions wherever possible. Work at creating correlations between your collaboration tools and transaction infrastructure. For example, you can establish practices that require any chat or online conference that references an emerging transaction should include a unique ID identifying that transaction. (Better yet, have the system enforce this.) Conversely, transactions should contain references to discussion threads or Wiki entries hosting the collaboration supporting the business decision transacted.

Better yet, migrate toward the new generation of workflow systems that are described as "case handling" systems.[20] Case handling systems integrate structure data, unstructured discussion, and process state in a single-metaphor environment. Case handling integrates collaboration and transaction principles in their core architecture. As always, the rule is in the tool.

---

20. "Case Handling: A New Paradigm for Business Process Support," Wil van der Aalst et. al., This is a good primer on the emerging case handling systems. http://is.tm.tue.nl/staff/wvdaalst/publications/p252.pdf

36

Use a Personal Touch with Executives Who Are New to Web Conferencing

As a web conferencing consultant and trainer, I often get asked, *"How can we avoid a glitch that causes a distraction from the success of our virtual meetings?"*

Henry Liebling is an expert at web conferencing. He is the co-founder of MoreVirtual.com and is the author of "The Web Conferencing Imperative for Collaboration, Productivity, and Training."

Throughout my career, I have noticed the importance of using a "personal touch" with people who are "new to something."

I still remember the fifteen minute 1:1 telephone training I received from the telephone sales person. I remember the technician who helped me the first time I connected my laptop to a projection system.

In 1992, I began learning about and using audio graphic conferencing (now called web conferencing). During this process, I discovered the University of Wisconsin was a leader in distance learning.

One factor to their success was taking away the "technical stress" of classroom professors who were becoming distance educators. The "newbie" distance teacher was able to rely on a technical person to handle all things technical. Before the virtual class was to start, the technical person would show up and set up the computer and modem. The fun part of this story is that many of the distance teachers became comfortable with the technical aspects by observing how it was done; they became self-sufficient and, after a while, they did not need the technical person to be with them in the same room.

As a web conferencing consultant and trainer, I often get asked, *"How can we avoid a glitch that causes a distraction from the success of our virtual meetings?"* I also hear this concern, *"I have invited an executive to participate in the web conference and I want to win his/her favor with these virtual meetings."*

Avoid Glitches and Give the Executive a Great Experience

Before the Virtual Meeting. Here are two things you can do before the actual virtual meeting. To me, these are "process steps" that need to be put into one's calendar. A personal touch takes a few extra minutes, but it paves the way for success.

Use a Personal Touch. Offer a personalized "trial run" with the executive. For example, several days before the virtual meeting, telephone the executive and work with him or her to practice the "join the web conference" procedure. If the executive is to speak to slides you will be presenting, bring up some slides and take a minute or two to practice and coordinate. If appropriate, practice some of the annotation tools. Ask questions and "listen up" to what's on the mind of the executive. My first-hand experience is that this approach wins favor with people who are new to web conferencing.

Get Help from the Executive's Assistant or Colleague. From time to time, I hear this complaint, *"I can't find the email invitation that contains the meeting link and the audio information."* I work with the executive's assistant or a colleague to ensure the executive has the join the meeting information when it is needed. One assistant rewrote the information onto a 3 x 5 card, handed the card to the executive, and told him, *"Put the card in your pocket and use it when you sit down at the computer."* A person "new to web conferencing" can also sit next to an experienced person and they can join the virtual meeting together.

By planning ahead when working with executives who are new to web conferencing, you accomplish important objectives:

- The executive has a very good experience with web conferencing.
- The web conference starts on time with minimum distractions.

Meeting these objectives helps to create winning attitudes about web conferencing.

37 There's More to Web Conferencing than Webinars

When it comes to using web conferencing software in one's work, it seems most people think vanilla and chocolate and not 31 flavors.

Henry Liebling is an expert at web conferencing. He is the co-founder of MoreVirtual.com and is the author of "The Web Conferencing Imperative for Collaboration, Productivity, and Training."

As a kid, I loved Carvel ice cream, vanilla and chocolate, in cones and in flying saucers. In later years, I was happy to discover Baskin-Robbins "31 Flavors" ice cream. I still remember how confused I first felt with their fantastic selection.

When it comes to using web conferencing software in one's work, it seems most people think vanilla and chocolate and not 31 flavors.

To me, a webinar is just one flavor. I think of a webinar as a type of Web Conference Virtual Meeting, similar to a seminar taught in a classroom. In short, a webinar usually informs and conveys information with some type of question and answer process between the audience and the presenter.

Are There Other Flavors of Web Conferencing?

In working with organizational development professionals, one of the audience members said, *"I'm here in Atlanta and my client needs my skills in France, but there is no travel budget and a webinar is not what they need from me."* She was asking, "Is there another web conferencing flavor for me?"

I taught her and the class how to use web conferencing to conduct a virtual force field analysis. (This type of analysis was originally developed by Kurt Lewin and is often used when planning and implementing a change program.)

A Vice President of sales said to me, *"Hey, we use webinars for lead generation, what else can we do with web conferencing?"*

Since high customer loyalty/retention was critical to the company's success, I taught him how to use web conferencing for collaborative account planning. This was cool because the customer had key stakeholders in multiple cities and the sales team was 100 percent virtual in different cities. Another flavor!

I visualize the way I want a face-to-face meeting to go and making this happen using web conferencing to support people who are separated geographically.

What Else Can You Do with Web Conferencing Software?

In a recent workshop, I provided a list of what people can do when they use web conferencing software.

- *Webinars* – inform or convey information with Q&A
- Demo a product and sell an idea, product or solution
- See, talk, listen, ask, type, involve, engage
- *Discuss* – in small and large groups and document agreements and actions to be taken
- Facilitate, plan and set goals or define a problem
- Give feedback, debrief, build consensus or make decisions
- *Manage* – people, projects, contracts, and budgets
- Present facts, analyze and critique
- Brainstorm (Ideation)
- Socialize, build rapport, and build relationships
- Set priorities, plan and coordinate
- Train, educate, coach, mentor
- Consult or provide expertise
- Create/edit content
- Create alignments and reduce silo thinking
- Provide/receive technical support
- *Account planning* – with your clients and your team
- Provide Organizational Development (OD) services, e.g., force field analysis

38 Persistence Is Critical

Tools that combine synchronous and asynchronous capabilities allow for collection and collaboration of integrated knowledge.

Henry Hon is co-founder and CEO of Berkeley, California, based software development firm Simulât, Inc. whose Vyew.com is a collaboration technology platform that unifies synchronous (real-time) plus asynchronous (always-on) collaboration techniques.

Persistence is the ability to have a document or object you put online, stay online and be available for others (who have access) at a different time. The ability to work with documents and each other over time is called asynchronous collaboration.

Real-time or synchronous collaboration tools on the other hand offer interactions that occur in real time (within 5 seconds, according to Collaborative Strategies). These real-time on-demand collaboration technologies such as WebEx, GoToMeeting, Live Meeting, etc. are great tools for real-time interactions. However, when the real-time interaction is completed (a web conference for example), the documents used in that web conference as well as any chat or other discussion disappear and no new knowledge is saved or available for reuse.

Our experience with working with virtual teams and workgroups is that they have the highest level of performance with a collaboration software platform, that combines both synchronous and asynchronous feature sets. Such tools should be able to support:

• Presentation authoring

- Web conferencing
- Chat and presence detection
- Simple document management
- Enhanced whiteboard and annotation
- Blogs and Wikis
- Forums or threaded discussions
- Web publishing features
- Group calendar
- Ability to display RSS feeds

These tools allow for collection and collaboration of integrated knowledge. The persistence gained allows the workgroup or community to glean from and build upon collective knowledge. Adding persistence allows your workgroup to not only meet online and to communicate in real time, but to build knowledge management capacities also.

Asynchronous capabilities allow you to harness the power of "social" networking for business. Social networks (Facebook, Myspace, LinkedIn, etc.) are popular with consumers but have not been widely adopted by the enterprise. One reason is that in the consumer world networking is based on personality or who you know. In the business world, it is more relevant to network around a particular topic or specific content.

For example a facilities person at Company A uses a wide variety of sub-contractors to keep up their physical plant. After a few initial meetings most of the work is no longer done in person, and a persistent space is created to store all the relevant documents and conversations. Over time quite a knowledge base is built up about Company A's facilities, maintenance, and improvements. Other personnel at Company A, who are not part of facilities, may get access to this persistent space which allows them to get up to speed, learn, and contribute to the projects more quickly. These users can invite other interested parties and the Network Effect is realized.

These combined collaboration tools also support the way people work in a more natural way allowing them to move between these states as they progress through their day. It prevents the use of multiple tools, jumping from one tool to the other, which is also inefficient and makes the interaction much more complex.

39 Use Visual Technologies for Collaboration

Over the last decade these systems have been getting easier, and significantly less expensive.

Because so much of the information we get in an interaction with one or more people is visual, why are not videoconferencing technologies seen as the most critical of collaboration technologies and used more widely?

Every year for the last decade has been decried by pundits and analysts alike as "the year of videoconferencing." And yet it has not happened. Yes, more and more there are cameras built into all of our gadgets (smart phones, laptop computers, etc.). The amount of user based content produced is staggering; just look at YouTube sometime. However, this is all streaming technology and not interactive video conferencing.

For many years room-based systems from the likes of Polycom, Tandberg, and Sony, were what could be found in most enterprise board rooms. These systems could be expensive and cost from $30–$120k, and the rooms are fully booked during working hours. However, many of the systems in these rooms were so complex that an engineer or IT support person was needed to make sure the technology worked correctly. Over the last decade these systems have been getting easier, and significantly less expensive.

But on the other end of the visual technology spectrum is telepresence. This is essentially a high-end room based system with fixed positions for the participants, cameras and lighting in a special room that gives the illusion of extending into an identical room thousands of miles away.

These systems were first introduced a few years ago by HP (Halo), Polycom (RealPresence), and Cisco (TelePresence) and cost about $250–$300k per room (and you need at least two). Additionally, these rooms only worked within and not between vendors.

I once asked a COO client, who flew almost 200 days a year why he was interested in spending so much money for telepresence systems. His reply was twofold: it would get him off of an airplane, make him more productive and give him back some of his life; and even though his company did build their own web cams, the telepresence system was the only one he would trust when he talked with the head of production for their factory in China and asked "if the factory was going to meet the production goals for this quarter."

The reason for trusting the telepresence system was that he wanted to be able to see the factory manager's facial expression to see if he was looking down at his feet when he was replying to the COO's question. The COO knew that the factory manager came from a culture that tried not to engage in direct conflict (a high touch culture) and that a "yes" answer did not always mean "yes." He needed to look for other visual cues to accurately determine the factory manager's answer. The COO's rationalization for the high price of these systems was that even if it saved him a few trips to China, the system paid for itself very quickly. If it helped avoid production delays and helped in the coordination of the supply chain it paid for itself even more quickly.

What I learned from this and other experiences with videoconferencing technologies was:

- Get the technology appropriate to your level of interaction and intimacy (teleconferencing is a lot more intimate than a web cam conference).
- No video technologies are easy, no matter what the vendor tells you! Make sure you have adequate technical support, or the interactions will all be focused on the technology that is not working instead of the work itself!
- Video is not appropriate for all interactions. Often project or status updates are fine to give through text or, if interactivity is needed, through a web conferencing tool.
- Video has more impact on bandwidth and infrastructure than any other collaboration technology, especially if you are using multiple video streams (i.e. seeing the picture of more than one person on your screen).

40

It Is Easier to Move Bits than Butts

With the economic crisis and volatile gas prices, many companies have instituted "travel restrictions" that allow only a few people to fly, and only when they absolutely have to and can show no other way to accomplish their goal.

Joan Vandermate is the Vice President of Marketing, Video Solutions Group, Polycom, Inc. She looks at the value of video conferencing in today's economic climate.

It is easier, faster, and more cost effective to move information rather than people. F2F interactions are still critical, of course, especially at the beginning of a relationship, for the establishment of trust and team dynamics. Video conferencing technologies, which are becoming as easy to use as a telephone, are now being incorporated into everyday business communications. Desktop and room-based video systems called "telepresence" rooms (offered by Polycom, Cisco, HP, and others) have helped many organizations eliminate much of the travel required for meetings, saving travel time and costs while boosting productivity.

With the economic crisis and volatile gas prices, many companies have instituted "travel restrictions" that allow only a few people to fly, and only when they absolutely have to and can show no other way to accomplish their goal. Below is a list of several ways video conferencing can be used to not only cut costs, but increase the transparency and participation that are integral parts of the Web 2.0 philosophy.

- **Entertainment 2.0:** It used to be that finding talent for commercials, TV shows, and movies required months of in-depth researching and back and forth travel between wherever you found the talent and the directors in NYC or LA. It used to be that an actor's ability to convey human emotion and motivation was so critical that it could only be done F2F. But high definition, interactive video conferencing has forever changed the casting business.

- **Head Hunting 2.0:** Much like casting actors, corporate recruiters have to pull talent from all over the world in a search for a candidate to fill a specific position. This can often take months and be very expensive. But using HD video recruiters today can interview many candidates through video and only select the top 2–3 to fly to meet the hiring company in person. This not only saves time and money for the interviewing company, but often provides a positive experience for those being interviewed and makes more talent available to the hiring company.

- **Trial and Punishment 2.0:** Criminal justice systems nationwide are saving *hundreds of millions* of dollars by taking a page from the corporate playbook around the use of video conferencing technologies. Not only is it less expensive, but it is also safer (less prisoner transport). One county in Michigan saves $4.2 million annually by processing inmates from arrest through arraignment—directly from their holding cell—through the use of video conferencing equipment. What was a 10-day process now takes just hours, and is safer. Prosecutors, law enforcement, corrections, and the courts can access records and track cases online. A simple click on a web page can initiate a F2F video conference from any courtroom to any officer, prosecutor and holding cell in the county.

- **Transparency in Civil Government:** Video has come to government in civic matters, too. Recently, New York mandated that its state agencies post videos of their public meetings on the Internet. This is just part of the transparency that is a hallmark of Web 2.0 technologies, and is starting to be demanded by civilian populations that want to know (in detail) what the politicians representing them are doing.

- **Medicine 2.0:** At its core, the modern healthcare system is collaboration between medical service providers and patients. It requires a tight orchestration of people, processes and technologies…yet it remains an intimate, trust-based human interaction. "Telemedicine" or the use of HD video technologies instead of personal visits allows doctors to see patients regardless of location, yet with the intimacy of an in-person visit. Stroke patients only have a 3-hour window to be treated before significant brain damage occurs. The doctor not only needs to see the patient, but to see how they react to specific tests that tell the doctor where the blood clot may be. Because this often requires expert diagnosis, local doctors can enlist the aid of these experts through video to give their stroke patients the best care at a reasonable price.

41

Pioneers Collaborate in Virtual Worlds

One of these companies, StatoilHydro (headquartered in Norway), sees interesting opportunities on this front as part of its initiative they refer to as "industrial gaming."

Eilif Trondsen has worked at SRI for many years and believes that the future of work will focus on collaboration and increasingly on virtual teams. And this type of collaboration can be more effective, efficient, and, yes, even fun, when done in an immersive 3D environment, i.e. virtual world.

Early surveys of those using Virtual Worlds (VW) point to the fact that "collaborative work" is one of the major uses of virtual worlds today (2008). Although many people use VW for entertainment purposes an early survey by SRI shows about 70 percent of those that do work in VW believe VW aids in collaboration and working in distributed teams (Virtual Worlds @ Work initiative of SRI Consulting Business Intelligence (http://www.sric-bi.com/vww)—in early 2008 of 77 active users of virtual worlds (and members of four different communities of practice focused on virtual worlds)—found that 70 percent of the survey respondents saw virtual worlds to hold "significant potential to improve effectiveness and/or efficiency of collaborative work, for instance among virtual teams of distributed workers)."

In 2008 there are about 80 different VW noted Sara de Freitas, who did a recent report on VW called "Serious Virtual Worlds: A Scoping Study

(Nov. 2008). There are another 100 planned for 2009. She also divides VW into five different categories based on primary function and use:

1. Role play worlds (World of Warcraft, Everquest, and Guild Wars)
2. Social worlds (SecondLife, Cyworld, ActiveWorlds, Habbo Hotel, Club Penguin(kids))
3. Training worlds (Forterra's OLIVE)
4. Mirror worlds (Google Earth, Planet Earth, and Unype)
5. Working worlds (Project Wonderland of Sun Microsystems and IBM's Metaverse)

There are many different forms of collaboration in these different types of VW; A major project commissioned by IBM and done by Seriosity (involving Byron Reeves, Tom Malone and Tony O'Driscoll) examined various forms of collaboration taking place in Massively Multiplayer Online Games (such as World of Warcraft), and what leadership skills players gained from playing these types of games (An article, Leadership Online Labs, based on this project appeared in the May 2008 issue of Harvard Business Review). Some of their key findings include:

- Business success is increasingly dependent on the effectiveness of global teams assembled for short-term objectives and composed of people with highly diverse backgrounds, many of whom meet entirely via electronic media. These conditions mirror the experiences of millions of players competing and collaborating every day in games such as World of Warcraft, a title published by Blizzard Entertainment.
- Leadership behavior that emerges in the game setting has many of the desirable properties of leadership in business. Some of the game conditions that contribute to this success include a framework that encourages risk-taking, fluid role changes between leading and following, and experimentation with a variety of economic incentives.

Being present via one's avatar in an immersive world opens up intriguing opportunities for future collaborative work. One of these companies, StatoilHydro (headquartered in Norway), sees interesting opportunities on this front as part of its initiative they refer to as "industrial gaming." In the next few years we are likely to see growing numbers of small and large companies recognizing that they can save money and time on travel by using virtual worlds, and in the process transform boring meetings into more interesting, engaging and productive collaborative sessions.

42

These Are My Rules. What Are Yours?

The goal of this book was both to prove a point about collaboration, and to get contributions from others. I relied on my social networks and communities to provide 32 rules out of the 42 in the book. The idea of the book is one of collected wisdom, rather than just the knowledge and experience of one man, no matter how much experience he has and what he knows about collaboration.

I think the experiment was successful. What about you? Did you learn anything from any of the rules or the book in total? The instructions I gave each of the contributing authors (and which I took to heart myself) were, "If a person you know picked up the book for just a few minutes and read just one rule, would they be able to get something of great value from it?"

My other goal was to have a book that was simple enough to read, that anyone (including my Mom) could read and get value from. My first two books (published by Prentice-Hall in the 90's) were each about 650 pages long and were used as textbooks for colleges and graduate school classes as they were some of the first books on Groupware to appear. However, those books were both out of date before they were even published.

My next book, and my first with HappyAbout, came out last year and is called "Collaboration 2.0" and is a collaboration between Stewart Levine (who also wrote 4 rules for this book) and myself. My goal with that book was not only to take a holistic look (people, process, and technology) at collaboration, but to provide the information in a much more palatable form. True to form, my Mom did say it was more readable.

My goal with this book was to make something that was of value, yet could be read by anyone, not just someone familiar with all the technology and jargon. It is my hope that my Mom will find this book much more readable and of greater value. Although anyone can read the book and get value from it, the particular audience it was written for was for more of an enterprise audience trying to deal with teams distributed across continents struggling to deal with the complexities of both the technology and their interpersonal interactions. To this audience, I hope you find this book of collected wisdom to be of great value.

My eventual goals for this or my next book are twofold, and diametrically opposed: To get a seminal article on collaboration into Harvard Business Review (HBR), and to have a book that is easy enough to read that you could buy it in an airport book store, off the shelf with only a few seconds to read the caption on the back cover. A noble goal for my next book, as I believe to make something that is complex seem easy and simple takes a lot of thought and work. My hat is off to those collaboration vendors that have been able to do this.

I am sure that after reading through the rules in this book, you have some of your own that you would like to formulate. If you would like them to see a public and interested audience, please send them to me at: _davidc@collaborate.com_ and I will see if they can be published either in my "Collaboration Blog" or a special blog I am developing that is just for rules about collaboration and features a new rule every week. Again, I look forward to your contributions and collaboration.

About the Author

David Coleman, Founder and Managing Director of Collaborative Strategies (CS), http://www.collaborate.com, has been involved with groupware, collaborative technologies, knowledge management (KM), online communities, and social networks since 1989. He is a thought leader, frequent public speaker, industry analyst, and author of books and magazine articles on these topics. His comments and analyses are most frequently found in the "Collaboration Blog." http://www.collaborate.com. He has worked with a wide range of collaboration vendors including IBM/Lotus, Microsoft, Macromedia, Adobe, Intuit, EMC, and Oracle, and helped them with strategy, positioning, or demand generation projects. He also works with end-user organizations to help them select collaboration technologies, and most recently has been working with them on "collaborative consolidation" within the enterprise, building online communities and creating a variety of social networks. David also works with distributed teams (across organizational boundaries) to transform them into high-performance teams. He can be reached at: davidc@collaborate.com or at (415) 282-9197.

Other Books by David Coleman:

Groupware Technology and Applications, Prentice Hall, 1995

Groupware: Collaborative Strategies for Corporate LANs and Intranets, Prentice Hall, 1997

Collaboration 2.0 (with Stewart Levine), Happy About Press, February 2008

In "42 Rules for Successful Collaboration" David Coleman wrote Rules: 1, 3, 23, 25, 27, 28, 30, 3, 39, and 42.

Contributors to this Book

This appendix contains those authors that have contributed to this book.

William (Bill) Black (Rule 16) William (Bill) Black is National Director of Strategic Business Solutions for Haworth and is located in Calgary, Alberta, Canada. A Quantity Surveyor originally hailing from Edinburgh, Scotland, he studied at Napier University, while serving an apprenticeship with local firm Gibson & Simpson. Bill received his B.Sc. in 1987, and moved to Canada in June 1991. After several years in the construction industry in a consulting role and then with a commercial sub trade Bill joined Haworth in October of 1999. In addition to his strategic work with Haworth on projects around the country Bill is also a frequent speaker at National events for ASID, AIA, IIDA, NAIOP, CORENET, BOMA, IFMA and others on the subjects of Sustainable, High Performance Buildings, the Value of Design and Strategic Real Estate Solutions. Bill is also a LEED Accredited Professional and in early April 2008 was one of 250 Canadians who were personally trained by Al Gore in Montreal as certified presenters of the Climate Change Program.

William (Bill) Black, B.Sc.
LEED AP
National Director,
Strategic Business Solutions,
Haworth,
10 Smed Lane SE,
Calgary, AB Canada, T2C 4P5
Phone: 403 203 6158
Mobile: 403 830 7477
Email: Bill.Black@haworth.com

Gabriel Blanc-Laine (Rule 22) Gabriel Blanc-Laine has over 20 years of international sales and marketing experience within the high-tech industry for a range of businesses from start-ups to large public companies (Texas Instruments, Sun Microsystems, Sybase, Vivendi/Cegetel). Recent accomplishments include driving Tekelec (NASDAQ TKLC) Software Business Unit revenue from $18 million in 2004 to $75 million in 2006 as VP of Product Management & Marketing. Previously Gabriel revitalized the sales and marketing efforts of Steleus, a French start-up acquired by Tekelec in October 2004 for $56M, and developed business in Eastern Europe, Asia, Middle East, and Africa. In 2000, he participated as VP Marketing and International Business Development to the European launch of SellingVision, a SaaS/Sales Force Automation startup.

Gabriel Blanc-Laine
VP Sales & Marketing,
Qtask, Inc.,
http://www.Qtask.com
Office: +1 (818) 562 840 x340
Mobile: +1 (818) 667 7338
LinkedIn: http://www.linkedin.com/in/GBlancLaine
Twitter: http://twitter.com/GBlancLaine

Shawn Callahan (Rule 15) Anecdote uses innovative storytelling (business narrative) and collaboration techniques to help large organisations redesign and improve the way people learn, share information and retain knowledge in an organisation. Their techniques are based on a belief that stories are fundamental to the way people communicate, learn, negotiate and solve problems. Anecdote's collaboration techniques, such as setting up communities of practice and peer-assist programs, are improving the way engineers share vital procedural and design information to achieve productivity gains. They regularly blog at http://www.anecdote.com.au and their work in collaboration has been published in *Business Review Weekly* and other mainstream media. The people we collaborate with in delivering projects, our Anecdote associates (http://www.anecdote.com.au/associates.php), are recognized thought leaders in their fields.

Shawn Callahan
Founding Director,
Anecdote Pty Ltd.
Email: Shawn@anecdote.com.au

Rachel Casanova (Rule 20) With over fourteen years of experience in corporate environments, Rachel Casanova has a solid background in helping companies transform their real estate assets in ways that reinforce long-term business strategies and corporate culture. Rachel has practiced as part of the client team, from the furniture manufacturer's perspective, and currently in the interior architectural and design arena. She graduated from Cornell University with a B.S. in Design and Environmental Analysis.

Rachel Casanova
LEED® AP
Senior Associate,
Perkins & Will,
Ideas + buildings that honor the broader goals of society,
http://www.perkinswill.com
215 Park Ave. South,
New York, NY 10003
Phone: 212 251 7054
Fax: 212 251 7111
Email: rachel.casanova@perkinswill.com

Joy Gilfilen (Rule 11) Joy Gilfilen blogs at JoyThinks.com and is the author of *Flipping the Joy Switch, Inner-Outer Collaboration* and *Take Charge of Your Destiny*. Joy is a consultant, keynote speaker and a 'ReVisionary'. She will help you review your vision with an eye to future change, and the current market...and will help you look at alternative routes to achievement. Joy believes that collaborative entrepreneurism is the new frontier of opportunity. Joy is the founder of UnitingCreatives.com, a marketplace and networking center to empower people, projects, and companies who are striving to improve our environmental, social, and global future.

Joy Gilfilen
Phone: 360 647 2831
Email: GiJoy@comcast.net

Henry Hon (Rule 38) Henry Hon is co-founder and CEO of Berkeley, California, based software development firm *Simulât*, Inc. whose Vyew.com is rapidly emerging as the market-leader in an important collaboration technology platform category that unifies synchronous (real-time) plus asynchronous (always-on) collaboration techniques. Vyew's unified collaboration platform has been adopted by over 100,000 users worldwide and major corporate, education and government organizations. Mr. Hon was previously EVP at Authenex, CEO at ShopD, EVP at Ramax, CEO at Visionex, and EVP at Dahon. Mr. Hon has an B.S. in Industrial Engineering Operations Research from University of California at Berkeley. Simulat, Inc., prior to focusing exclusively on unified collaboration and the Vyew platform, was building simulations for education and training for large tech companies such as Microsoft, Nortel, and Websense. Before that Mr. Hon led complex systems development projects centered on chip-level design and both hardware and software. Mr. Hon's diverse experience helps mold Vyew into a collaboration tool that can be adopted across many industries.

Henry Hon
CEO,
Vyew,
Vyew.com
2180A Dwight Way,
Berkeley, CA, 94704
Phone: (800) 594 4559
Email: henry@simulat.com

Tim Hughan (Rule 14) Tim Hughan is Director of Marketing at Altus Learning, responsible for executing Altus' product, services and company vision in all customer and product communications. Tim brings over 15 years experience delivering successful and compelling marketing programs to a variety of audiences.

Prior to joining Altus Learning, Tim worked for a variety of companies including Apple, Hyperion (now Oracle), Schlumerger, Solix and Benjamin/Cumming Publishing in both individual contributor and management roles in marketing communications, advertising, and lead generation roles. Tim is an alumnus of CSU, Chico and holds a degree in Instructional Design.

Tim Hughan
Director of Marketing,
Altus Learning Systems,
http://www.altuscorp.com
16450 Los Gatos Blvd,
Suite 207,
Los Gatos, CA 95032
Office: 408 395 9154
Direct: 408 884 1480/360 647 2831
Mobile: 408 202 4503
Email: thughan@altuscorp.com

Vadim Katcherovski (Rule 33) Vadim Katcherovski is the founder and CEO of Logic Software Inc. which makes easyprojects.net. He has been in the software business for a surprisingly long time for a man of his age.

Vadim Katcherovski
Logic Software Inc.,
http://www.easyprojects.net
Phone: + 1 416 907 9944
Fax: + 1 928 752 3905
Email: vadim@easyprojects.net

Kjetil Kristensen (Rule 21) Kjetil Kristensen is the Principal Consultant of Kristensen Consulting (KC). KC is an independent, research-based consultancy that provides guidance on collaborative strategies and effective, reliable collaborative infrastructures and work practices that improve collaborative performance. Kristensen has a Ph.D. in collaborative engineering from the Norwegian University of Science and Technology. He speaks and publishes internationally on a broad range of topics related to collaboration and collaborative innovation.

Kjetil Kristensen, Ph.D.
Kristensen Consulting
http://www.kristensenconsulting.com
Phone: +47 92615008
Email: kjetil@kristensenconsulting.com
Skype: kjetilkristensen

Rob Langejans (Rule 13) Rob Langejans a Senior Sales Coach/Consultant for Haworth since 2004, is an expert in helping business leaders communicate clear messages that inspire. Prior to coming to Haworth, Rob was an account manager and communications consultant for a Michigan-based firm where he worked with organizations such as Coca-Cola, Kellogg's, URS, Herman Miller, Stryker Medical, Steelcase, Clarian Health Partners, and Johnson Controls. In addition to creating original training sessions on business topics, Rob holds certifications from several leading training organizations. Rob has coached business leaders in North America, Mexico, and Europe and holds a Bachelor's degree in Psychology from Calvin College.

Rob Langejans
HAWORTH, Inc.,
One Haworth Center,
Holland, MI 49423
Phone: 616 393 1311
Email: rob.langejans@haworth.com

Stewart Levine (Rules 6, 7, 8, 10, and 19) Stewart Levine is a "Resolutionary." His innovative work with "Agreements for Results" and his "Cycle of Resolution" are unique. "Getting to Resolution: Turning Conflict into Collaboration" was an Executive Book Club Selection; featured by Executive Book Summaries; named one of the 30 Best Business Books of1998; and called "a marvelous book" by Dr. Stephen Covey. It has been translated into Russian, Hebrew and Portuguese. "The Book of Agreement" has been endorsed by many thought leaders, called "more practical" than the classic "Getting to Yes," and named one of the best books of 2003 by CEO Refresher (http://www.Refresher.com). He consults to many government agencies, Fortune 500 companies, professional associations and organizations of all sizes. He teaches communication and collaboration skills for the American Management Association. You can find more information about him at http://www.ResolutionWorks.com. You can reach him at ResolutionWorks@msn.com or 510-777-1166.

Stewart L. Levine, Esq., Resolutionary
Author:
- Getting to Resolution
- The Book of Agreement
- The Cycle of Resolution in the Change Handbook
- Collaboration 2.0, http://www.happyabout.info/collaboration2.0.php

Resolution Works,
http://www.resolutionworks.com
Phone: 510 777 1166
Mobile: 510 814 1010
Email: Resolutionworks@msn.com

Henry Liebling (Rules 36 and 37) Henry E. Liebling is co-founder of http://www.MoreVirtual.com. He provides consulting, training, and coaching to help people get better use of web conferencing and related collaboration tools. Henry is author of four books on web conferencing:

1. The Web Conferencing Imperative for Collaboration, Productivity, and Training
2. The Web Conferencing IDEA BOOK for Marketing and Sales
3. The Web Conferencing IDEA BOOK for Training and Human Resources
4. The Web Conferencing IDEA BOOK for Government

Henry E. Liebling
Phone: 678 777 6960
Email: hliebling@morevirtual.com

Pat Lupica (Rule 18) Pat is a Ph.D. candidate at the International School of Management in Paris, France, and holds a Masters in Supply Chain Management (SCM) from the University of San Diego (USD). Activities include teaching Supply Chain and Operations Management at USD, a publication reviewer for the Institute for Supply Management, and a contract SCM subject matter expert for John Wiley & Sons. Pat is also the president of LNK Consulting, a value chain integration company that provides a practical and comprehensive framework to eliminate or greatly minimize silo centric performance.

Pat Lupica
President,
LNK Consulting,
http://supplychainexperts.ning.com
Mobile: 760 688 6100
Email: pat@lnkconsulting.net

Jason Pratt (Rule 12) Jason Pratt is a Collaboration Subject Matter Expert at Autodesk, Inc. He's previously been in software development, project management and product management at Autodesk, and throughout his career has worked for (or served on boards of) a variety of Internet and virtual reality software companies. Since 1994, Jason has always been involved in one way or another in the Internet software space. Jason holds an MBA from Duke University and a Bachelor of Science in Architecture from the University of Texas at San Antonio. He resides in Austin, TX, with his wife Kelly, and children Megan and John.

Jason Pratt
Sr. Subject Matter Expert, Collaboration,
Autodesk, Inc.
Phone: 512 371 3013
Email: Jason.pratt@autodesk.com

Eric Richert (Rule 9) Eric Richert is Principal of 8 Corners Consulting, a practice focused on the support of knowledge-based work. 8 Corners builds on Eric's years of experience in creating, developing, and managing pioneering work environments for Sun Microsystems, Inc. He co-founded Sun's Open Work Solutions Group in 1997 and founded 8 Corners Consulting in 2007.

Eric received his MBA from the University of California at Berkeley and his Master of Architecture degree from Syracuse University. He is an active charter member of the New Ways of Working Network. (http://www.newwow.net)

Eric Richert
Phone: 650 854 7573
Mobile: 650 380 2008
Email: eric.richert@gmail.com

Jason Rothbart (Rule 24) Jason Rothbart is the Vice President of Customer Success at GroupSwim. He focuses on acquiring customers and making them successful. He is an experienced executive and provides consultative expertise for our customers. Jason has worked in the software and management consulting industry for 15 years. He ran Professional Services at newScale, McKesson and SEVEN prior to joining GroupSwim. He also held management positions with Deloitte Consulting, Ernst & Young and Commerce One. Jason received a Bachelor of Arts in English from UCLA and a Master in Business Administration and a Master in Public Health from Emory University in Atlanta, Georgia. Jason occasionally writes for ReadWriteWeb, one of the largest tech blogs in the world.

Jason Rothbart
Vice President,
Customer Success
Phone: 415 254 9737
Email: Jason@groupswim.com

Audrey Scarff (Rule 32) Audrey Scarff is a freelance consultant with expertise in web, intranet and online collaboration. Projects have involved high profile brands such as Shell International, HBOS, Alliance Boots, United Nations, Fairfax, and Telstra. She has helped hundreds of clients achieve their internal communication goals through solid online strategies backed up by the functionality provided by Intranet DASHBOARD. She has an M.A. in Virtual Communication, is on the Microsoft Partner Research Panel, and is the Director of Communication for the International Association of Business Communicators (IABC) Europe & Middle East Region, http://europe.iabc.com.

Audrey Scarff
eCommunications Consultant,
iCite & Intranet DASHBOARD,
http://www.intranetdashboard.com
Director of Communications,
IABC Europe Middle East,
Skype Auds06,
85 Tottenham Court Rd, London, W1T 4TQ
Phone: +44 0207 268 3772
Fax: + 44 0207 268 3100
Mobile: +44 07857 731 221
Email: audrey.scarff@intranetdashboard.com

Sheryl R. Sever (Rule 29) Sheryl R. Sever is an organizational learning consultant and compelling presenter with over 15 years experience developing and leading communication and leadership seminars to professionals from over 40 countries on four different continents.

She is passionate about activating human potential to facilitate transformation. She speaks and writes regularly about business trends, social change and innovation in the workplace. With entrepreneurial efficiency, fresh perspectives, and powerful implementation, she brings a sustainable, strategic solution oriented approach to marketing, product development, leadership, organizational effectiveness, and professional development.

Sheryl is an expert at change management, very motivated by the creativity, growth and wealth of opportunities inherent in the cycles of change.

Sheryl R. Sever
Founder: Cross Currents Communications,
Organizational Learning & Leadership
Marketing & Business Development
Training & Instructional Design
San Francisco Bay Area
Office: 510 336 9161
Mobile: 415 713 7727
http://www.sherylsever.com
http://www.linkedin.com/in/sherylangelina

Jane E. Smith (Rule 5) Jane E. Smith is the founder and President of LiSimba Consulting Services, Inc. LiSimba's work centers on **"Building Relationships for International Business Success."** She is a graduate of the William Mitchell College of Law, St. Paul, Minnesota, University of Texas at Denton, Texas, where she earned an M.Ed., Macalester College, including study at the Facultad de Filosofia Y Letras, University of Madrid, Spain, and two years reading ancient history and theology at Wycliffe Hall, Oxford University, Oxford, England, through the WEST Course. She is a global executive coach guiding executives to get to know themselves culturally and understand those with whom they work. She presents small and large group seminars for half a day up to three days, focusing on one or more of these topics: minimizing cultural risk in our global work environment; understanding how trust is created and functions in each culture; and creating client specific culturally appropriate conflict resolution models. Some of her writings and presentations include: "Minimizing Risk: Best Practices in Managing Cross Cultural Concerns in Global Contracting," a chapter in *The ABA Guide to International Business Negitiations, Third Edition*, April 2009; "The Maquiladora System as a Bridge Between the United States and Mexico," International Business Law News, Minnesota State Bar Association; the online simulation, "Managing Cross Cultural Concerns in Global Contracting," in collaboration with the IACCM; "The International Aspect of Post Merger/Acquisition Integration: Setting Strategic and Tactical Priorities to Capture the Value of the Deal," written and presented for Executive Enterprises. Her clients are Fortune 500 corporations, mid size businesses, law firms, and small businesses.

Jane E. Smith, Esq.
LiSimba Consulting Services, Inc.,
http://www.lisimba.com
3305 Eagle Bluff Road,
Minneapolis, Minnesota 55364 USA
Phone: 612 802 1240/952 472 6750
Fax: 952 472 2681

John Tibbetts (Rule 35) John Tibbetts is a software architect and active developer. For the past 21 years, through his consulting company Kinexis, he has helped enterprises and vendors improve efficiency and increase reuse by implementing coherent software architectures for their applications and products. He has served as mentor for development teams, provided thought leadership to management, and advised on new-technology adoption. Clients have ranged from Fortune 500 companies to startups. He was a columnist for InformationWeek magazine, and he writes and speaks widely.

John Tibbetts
Phone: 415 558 9277
Email: John.tibbetts@kinexis.com

Eilif Trondsen SRI (Rule 41) Eilif Trondsen, Ph.D., is the Research and Program Director of Virtual Worlds @ Work, (VWW), a research consortium focused on 3D immersive environments, at SRI Consulting Business Intelligence (SRIC-BI) in Menlo Park, California. The focus area of his research and consulting at SRIC-BI—a spin-out of SRI International (formerly Stanford Research Institute)—is the use of technology for business performance improvement and learning. He has 29 years' experience at SRIC-BI and at SRI International, leading or contributing to a variety of projects for U.S. and foreign clients in the private and public sectors. For ten years, Eilif held the position of Research Director of the Business Intelligence Program (now the Scan program) at SRI and currently leads VWW (http://www.sric-bi.com/vww). In his tenure at SRI and SRIC-BI, Eilif has given numerous presentations on various eCommerce, eLearning, and virtual worlds topics at conferences and to SRI clients around the world. Eilif has also the author and co-author of numerous publications on eCommerce, eLearning, and virtual world topics.

Eilif Trondsen, Ph.D.
Director, Virtual Worlds @ Work
Co-chair, Virtual Worlds SIG of SDForum,
SRI Consulting Business Intelligence,
http://www.sric-bi.com/,
333 Ravenswood Avenue,
Menlo Park, CA, 94025
Phone: 650 859 2665
Fax: 650 859 4544
Email: etrondsen@sric-bi.com

Joan Vandermate (Rule 40) Joan Vandermate is Vice President of Marketing of Video Solutions at Polycom, responsible for positioning and marketing the company's visual communication and collaboration platforms, management applications, recording and streaming solutions, and security products. Prior to joining Polycom, Vandermate was Vice President of Product Management at Siemens Communications, where she held management positions in product marketing and product line management, including rollout responsibilities for Siemens HiPath IP softswitches and telephones. Before joining Siemens, Vandermate worked for more than a decade in the personal computing and internetworking industries. She has presented and moderated at various technology forums including VoiceCon, VON, Internet Telephony, Frost & Sullivan Executive summits, and Stanford University technology seminars.

Joan Vandermate
Vice President of Marketing,
Video Solutions Group, Polycom, Inc.
Phone: 925 924 6088
Email: Joan.Vandermate@polycom.com

Sandy Vosk (Rule 26) Sandy has over 25 years of experience successfully implementing business solutions through the effective use of technology. His broad background in Fortune 500 and leading international corporations includes application development, senior management, global project management, strategic consulting, as well as managing the sales of software and professional services.

In July 2003, Sandy founded ATS, Inc., where he is directly responsible for the management, operations and sales of professional services, targeted predominantly to global manufacturing, warehouse/distribution and logistics companies. Sandy has leveraged his management experience at companies such as PepsiCo, Mutual of NY, TNT Express Worldwide, Philips Electronics and Sybase iAnywhere Solutions to help companies including Lansdale Warehouse Co. Inc., CFC Logistics, Hermann Services, Inc. and Ozburn-Hessey Logistics to lower operational costs, reduce shipping errors and significantly improve productivity and customer service.

The key strategy at ATS is to recommend and implement supply chain solutions which improve profitability and performance through improved management of inventory, warehousing and shipping.

Sandy Vosk
President & CEO ATS, Inc.
Office: 732-617-7166
Mobile: 732-995-2355
Email: svosk@advantage-ts.com
www.allied-tracking.com
www.advantage-ts.com
http://supplychainexperts.ning.com

AJ Wacaser (Rule 34) AJ Wacaser is the founder and CEO of
PlanDone, Inc., a Web-based project collaboration services company
serving small-medium-sized businesses. Growing tired of missing
deadlines and incomplete projects, AJ developed PlanDone to help
companies complete their projects on time.

AJ has more than 15 years' experience working in public and private
software companies in desktop and web development. He has successfully managed numerous projects around the globe for nine years.

Previously, AJ was the Web Development Manager at Knowledge-
Point, a HR software company in Petaluma, California. He helped
guide development through the dot com boom/bust and helped many
small businesses with a suite of pay-per-use on-demand HR productivity tools such as HRTools.com, JobDescription.com, PerformanceRe-
view.com, and PersonnelPolicy.com.

AJ graduated from Augustana College, and earned a M.A. in Environmental Planning from the University of Illinois.

AJ Wacaser
Founder and CEO,
PlanDone,
765 Baywood Dr. Suite 245,
Petaluma, CA 94954
Phone: (707) 338 3995
Email: aj@plandone.com

Leslie Yerkes (Rule 17) Leslie Yerkes is President of Catalyst Consulting Group, Inc. (http://www.changeisfun.com) an organizational development and change management consulting firm based in Cleveland, Ohio. Leslie's business goal is to help people create sustainable organizations. Her life goal is to create a framework in which people can draw on their own resources to find creative solutions. Her clients have included Chrysler Corporation, The Cleveland Clinic Foundation, United Church of Christ, ArcelorMittal Steel USA, and NASA. A subspecialty of Leslie's is making non-profits healthy and sustainable.

Leslie is a recognized consultant, author, and speaker throughout the United States and Europe. She is considered an expert in her field and is frequently quoted in the media. She is the author of "Fun Works: Creating Places Where People Love to Work" and "Motivation in the 21st Century without Kicks or Carrots," a co-author of "301 Ways to Have Fun at Work," "Beans: Four Principles for Running a Business in Good Times or Bad" and "They Just Don't Get It! Changing Resistance into Understanding." Her works have been translated into more than a dozen languages selling hundreds of thousands of copies worldwide.

A graduate of Wittenberg University and Case Western Reserve University, she has taught at John Carroll University and Baldwin Wallace College, and is on the faculty at the Weatherhead Dively Center of Executive Education, Case Western Reserve University.

Leslie Yerkes
President,
Catalyst Consulting Group, Inc.
http://www.changeisfun.com
12701 Larchmere Boulevard Suite 4A
Cleveland, Ohio 44120
Phone: 216 849 9551
Email: fun@catalystconsulting.net / Yerkes@bright.net

Jeff Young (Rules 2 and 4) Jeff Young is the founder of Coignite and helps individuals and organizations create the successful future they want for themselves. To accomplish this goal, Jeff facilitates collaborative learning communities that bring people together to help each other clarify the vision they have for the future and identify and hold each other accountable for the action and learning they need to grow into in order to become the future they seek.

Jeff Young
http:www.coignite.com
California: (415) 893 9282
Hawaii: (808) 554 8664
Mobile: (415) 595 8536
Email: jyoung@coignite.com

B Background Information

Blogging for Fun and Profit

A blog is essentially a single-threaded discussion where you can express your opinion and get feedback. Although a blog is an asynchronous collaboration tool, you can often get feedback quite rapidly, within minutes of posting the blog. I have been writing The Collaboration Blog for several years at http://www.collaborate.com. Blogs are generally in a template form, and there are some tools like TypePad[21] and Wordpress[22] that are very popular, and can offer some additional functionality through "add-ins."

Although blogs are single threaded they can be a 2-way conversation by linking to another's blog through tags (key words or phrases). Enterprise blogs have become a major PR tool today. An internal blogs is a way the CEO to talk with all the employees and get feedback. External blogs put a more personal face on the company and help build credibility with customers through transparency.

Blogs are not only used for PR, but have some of the following capabilities:

---

21. http://www.typepad.com
22. http://www.wordpress.org

- Blogs are searchable you can use services like Digg,[23] to see what others have tagged and said about a specific blog or blogger or an indexing service like Technorati.[24] You can also rate the story or blog.

- Blogs let you state your opinion, and get feedback, this can be a very powerful way to interact with your customers.

- Blogs can also help you to identify others with the same interest(s) through tags, or their responses to your or other topic related blogs.

- Blogs can be used as a business development tool to help you to find business partners or opportunities.

- Blogs can reduce email and provide more enterprise knowledge and are much less formal than other enterprise announcements.

Blogging is very popular today with millions of people doing it and is part of the "user created content" wave washing over the Internet. There is a new blog created every five seconds, with over 100,000 blog posts every day an almost 200 million blogs tracked by Technorati.[25] Like every other collaboration technology, content is critical and if not kept up on a regular basis the blog loses its readers. 60 percent of blogs that are created are abandoned. Today citizen reporters (bloggers) often report a story before the traditional media gets it.

Micro-blogging

Micro-blogging is a very short blog (140 characters like an SMS (text) message) that still carries your opinion, shares information with those who have the same interests, updates the appropriate people on a projects status, or can give your current location.

Twitter[26] is the most popular of the micro-blogging tools. There are about 2 million "tweets" (a message on twitter) a day. In Twitter you get to choose the people you follow and get to see their "tweets" every time they post one. Currently I am following about 200 people and have about 300 following me. If you want to follow me on Twitter I am "dcoleman100." There are lots of different Twitter clients, I use one that aggregates a lot of different types of Twitter information called Tweet-Deck.

---

23. http://digg.com/
24. http://www.technorati.com
25. http://technorati.com/blogging/state-of-the-blogosphere/
26. http://www.twitter.com/

There is an enterprise micro-blogging tool called Yammer[27] that was introduced in 2008, and with the popularity of Twitter expect to see more micro-blogging tools on the market. Micro-blogging can be very useful for:

- Letting people know what you are doing.
- Letting people know where you are (location) which plane you might be on or which airport or bar you are waiting in.
- Stream of consciousness reporting on an event while it is going on. I have done a number of these "tweet streams" from different conferences I have attended, and some of those who follow me have found this very useful when they can't attend the event themselves.

---

27. http://www.yammer.com

C Generational Collaboration

Some of the research we have done over the last year looks at different collaborative environments on the Internet and how the different genders and age groups rank and use features and functions in these environments.

- Email tool Popularity correlated with age

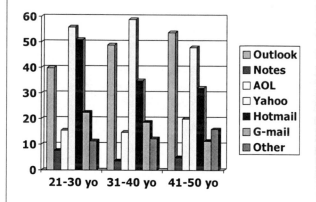

Outlook was popular with all age groups as was Yahoo mail, followed by G-Mail. In general email tools are used more by the 30–60 year olds, while the 20 year old prefer IM.

- How many emails/day correlated with age

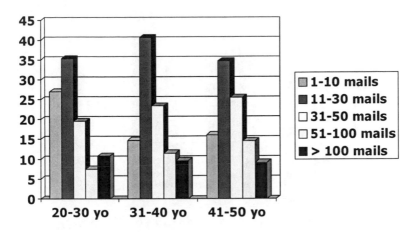

The number of email received each day was not very different between age groups with most all groups receiving about 100 emails a day.

- Email Messages Sent correlated with age

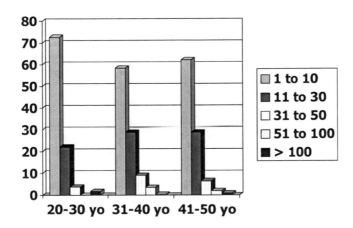

There was not much difference between different age groups and the number of emails they sent.

- Number of Online Groups Correlated with Age

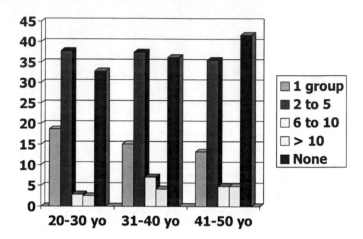

The older the age group the more people in the group were not in any social networking group.

42 Rules for Successful Collaboration

D

Another Teaming Challenge: Attention Management

Too Much Collaboration

A recent CNET article noted that the typical office worker is interrupted every three minutes by an email, IM, phone call, etc. If you are working on something creative, it takes about 8 minutes for our brains to get into that state. With all these distractions how is anyone able to get anything done.

The result, says Carl Honore, journalist and author of "In Praise of Slowness," is a situation where the digital communications that were supposed to make working lives run more smoothly are actually preventing people from getting critical tasks accomplished.

Chris Caposella a VP in the Microsoft Information Worker Business Unit says that "People are ultra connected. And you know what? Now they are starting to realize, 'Wow, I want to actually stop getting interrupted.'" Dan Russell, a researcher at IBM's Almaden Research Center, turns off the instant notification of email and only looks at email 2x a day and has cut the time he spends with email in half. Other organizations, like Veritas Software have implemented "no email Fridays." Employees can't email one another on Friday, but they are allowed to email customers or other parts of the storage company if they have to. The result? Workers spend more time connecting face to face.

A study by Hewlett-Packard earlier this year found that 62 percent of British adults are addicted to their email—checking messages during meetings, after working hours and on vacation. Half of workers felt a need to respond to emails immediately or within an hour, and one in five people reported being "happy" to interrupt a business or social gathering to respond to an email or phone message.

Even airlines are starting to offer broadband Internet access. So how will we be able to deal with this tidal wave of communications?

"With Microsoft Office 2007, we will do things to make it a lot easier for people to be more effective in the way they manage all of these communication mechanisms," Capossela said. IBM also is looking at solutions to manage scheduling for the next version of Lotus Workplace, part of IBM's collection of software that rivals Office.

But technology may not be the solution. Like many issues in collaboration it is the "people and process issues" that are the crux of the problem.

"The problem, Russell said, is that there are only certain types of tasks that humans are good at doing simultaneously. Cooking and talking on the phone go together fine, as does walking and chewing gum (for most people). But try and do three math problems at once, and you are sure to end up in frustration."

I have written a lot about what I call "attention management" and what everyone else calls "Continuous Partial Attention (term coined by Linda Stone)." Stowe has been blogging about this for months, and he and I have had a few discussions on the subject.

Basically, he believes that your social networks are your filter for information overload. If A likes it and I like and trust A, then I should like it. I agree with Stowe to a point, in that social networks only deal with part of the problem. I do not believe that you will be able to filter enough through these networks to stop the overwhelming of your bandwidth for both information and attention.

I believe that the problem needs to be attached also from the other direction. That is to augment a person's ability to "attend" to content and events. In my view of the future there are a variety of technology solutions that might help. But I don't think the scheduling tools that Microsoft and Lotus are building are it. I believe that you will need to multiply your bandwidth and attention by multiplying your self.

Some type of virtual agent that not only knows where you are, what you are doing and what collaboration programs or devices you have, but it also has a subset of your personality and is assigned to deal with specific types of tasks demanding your attention. For example, this virtual agent or avatar can deal with lower-level requests for attention and decisions around what to pick up at the grocery store. It knows your likes and dislikes, what is in the refrigerator and what is not, and you have empowered it to make those shopping decisions, and have the groceries delivered to your house at 6:00 pm (it knows your schedule and that you are due to have dinner with your family by 7:00 pm).

This leaves you free to deal with critical requests for your attention from your family, your boss, negotiating with a client, dealing with a crisis, etc. Since many fewer items fall into these "critical" categories your bandwidth and attention are on overwhelmed, and yet all of these other demands on your attention are also being satisfied.

In a recent article by Dr. Doree Seligmann from Avaya Research Labs http://tinyurl.com/cwxzdm,[28] she describes a virtual communications agent that is system agnostic and facilitates communication (or not) based on rules you give the system and what it knows about you and your devices. It is my belief that Avaya is building such a system as an abstracted layer that can be used by both developers and end-users. It is the closest to the Avatar or virtual agent that I described above that I have heard about.

However, I can't pay attention to everything, so if any of you out there know of other projects or services that will serve to augment my attention abilities I would love to hear about them!

---

28. 65.18.192.7/publication/newsletter/
publications_newsletter_august05.html

When Is MPD an Advantage?

In a recent talk I started my talk by asking the audience if anyone had MPD (multiple personality disorder). After a few nervous laughs and very few hands (besides mine) rose, I went on to talk about a future where the bandwidth for multimedia content was many times greater than what a person could process. With the advent of nano technology sensors starting to be built into all sorts of formerly inanimate objects, not only will your refrigerator be clamoring for your attention, but the road you're driving on, even your clothes all will want your attention.

The problem in the future is one of attention management, and when faced with the deluge of input and requests for interaction and collaboration, my premise was that a person would be able to split themselves into many parts, and assign specific parts to deal with each of these interaction streams. These parts would really be more like clones of you, or avatars, rather than actually splitting your personality or consciousness. You might have one that had some of your personality traits, and decision-making criteria that dealt with low-level issues like the refrigerator requesting that you buy milk, or dealing with spam (of various types). A more sophisticated clone might be authorized to deal with requests for basic information from you, while your main persona (you) could focus your attention on a negotiation with a business associate, or even a loved one.

I know this sounds like science fiction, but it is not so far fetched when you think about it. You have bots now like Google that go out and search the web to find all sorts of things you're looking for. There is currently BI (business intelligence) applications that can find specific types of information, and search programs that have semantic and context-based intelligence already built in. Is it such a stretch to see that you make some of these intelligent tools more permanent and more sophisticated? The more you add of your self to this agent, the more scope it may have to deal with various attention requests. If these agents have the ability to learn, then as they deal with more interactions, they should become capable of dealing with a wider scope of interactions, leaving you, the core intelligence/personality to deal with the tough stuff.

Although, I don't know of any collaboration companies working on such clones/agents/avatars, that does not mean they are not out there. If I can imagine a scenario like this, I am sure someone else has also, and unlike me, they are probably trying to find a solution to this emerging problem.

Write Your Own Rules

You can write your own 42 Rules book, and we can help you do it—from initial concept, to writing and editing, to publishing and marketing. If you have a great idea for a 42 Rules book, then we want to hear from you.

As you know, the books in the 42 Rules series are practical guidebooks that focus on a single topic. The books are written in an easy-to-read format that condenses the fundamental elements of the topic into 42 Rules. They use realistic examples to make their point and are fun to read.

Two Kinds of 42 Rules Books

42 Rules books are published in two formats: the single-author book and the contributed-author book. The single-author book is a traditional book written by one author. The contributed-author book (like *42 Rules for Working Moms*) is a compilation of Rules, each written by a different contributor, which support the main topic. If you want to be the sole author of a book or one of its contributors, we can help you succeed!

42 Rules Program

A lot of people would like to write a book, but only a few actually do. Finding a publisher, and distributing and marketing the book are challenges that prevent even the most ambitious of authors to ever get started.

At 42 Rules, we help you focus on and be successful in the writing of your book. Our program concentrates on the following tasks so you don't have to:

- **Publishing:** You receive expert advice and guidance from the Executive Editor, copy editors, technical editors, and cover and layout designers to help you create your book.

- **Distribution:** We distribute your book through the major book distribution channels, like Baker & Taylor and Ingram, Amazon.com, Barnes and Noble, Borders Books, etc.

- **Marketing:** 42 Rules has a full-service marketing program that includes a customized Web page for you and your book, email registrations and campaigns, blogs, webcasts, media kits and more.

Whether you are writing a single-authored book or a contributed-author book, you will receive editorial support from 42 Rules Executive Editor, Laura Lowell, author of *42 Rules of Marketing*, which was rated Top 5 in Business Humor and Top 25 in Business Marketing on Amazon.com (December 2007), and author and Executive Editor of *42 Rules for Working Moms*.

Accepting Submissions

If you want to be a successful author, we'll provide you the tools to help make it happen. Start today by answering the following questions and visit our website at http://superstarpress.com/ for more information on submitting your 42 Rules book idea.

Super Star Press is now accepting submissions for books in the 42 Rules book series. For more information, email info@superstarpress.com or call 408-257-3000.

Other Happy About Books

42 Rules™ of Social Media for Business'

This book is designed to help working professionals find social media that fits their business and get the most out of their social media presence.

Paperback:$19.95
eBook:$14.95

42 Rules™ for 24-Hour Success on LinkedIn

This book is a user-friendly guidebook designed to help you leverage the power of LinkedIn to build visibility, make connections and support your brand.

Paperback:$19.95
eBook:$14.95

I'M ON
LinkedIn
Now What???

JASON ALBA
FOREWORD BY BOB BURG

HappyAbout.info

Networking Online—Making LinkedIn Work for you!

This book explains the benefits of using LinkedIn and recommends best practices so that you can get the most out of it.

Paperback:$19.95
eBook:$14.95

I'm on
facebook
Now What???

JET, PROTECT PRIVACY, USE THE RIGHT APPLICATIONS, MARKET Y
BOOK, PROTECT THE COMPETITION, IMPROVE YOUR CAREER, GET
CATIONS, MARKET YOUR PRODUCTS AND SERVICES, PROTECT PRI
TITION, IMPROVE YOUR CAREER, GET NOTICED, TRACK YOUR LIFE,
UCTS AND SERVICES, PROTECT PRIVACY, TRACK YOUR LIFE, CREAT
TALK YOUR LIFE, CREATE THE KILLER PROFILE, FOLLOW THE COMP
TIN, PROTECT PRIVACY, USE THE RIGHT APPLICATIONS, MARKET Y
FOFILE, FOLLOW THE COMPETITION, IMPROVE YOUR CAREER, GET
CATIONS, MARKET YOUR PRODUCTS AND SERVICES, PROTECT PRO
UCTS AND SERVICES, PROTECT PRIVACY, TRACK YOUR LIFE, CREAT
BE, GET NOTICED, TRACK YOUR LIFE, ENHANCE PRODUCTIVITY, IM
RACE YOUR LIFE, CREATE THE KILLER PROFILE, FOLLOW THE COMP
TIT, USE THE RIGHT APPLICATIONS, MARKET YOUR PRODUCTS AN

JASON ALBA & JESSE STAY
Foreword by   Afterword by
Lee Lorenzen   Robert Scoble

HappyAbout.info

I'm on Facebook—Now What???

This book will help you come up with your own action strategy to get value out of Facebook.

Paperback:$19.95
eBook:$14.95

Purchase these books at Happy About
http://happyabout.info/
or at other online and physical bookstores.

A Message From Super Star Press™

Thank you for your purchase of this 42 Rules Series book. It is available online at: http://www.happyabout.info/42rules/successful-collaboration.php or at other online and physical bookstores. To learn more about contributing to books in the 42 Rules series, check out http://superstarpress.com.

Please contact us for quantity discounts at sales@superstarpress.com

If you want to be informed by email of upcoming books, please email bookupdate@superstarpress.com.

LaVergne, TN USA
23 May 2010
183621LV00002B/6/P